PHA(BU)LLUS

PHA(BU)LLUS

A Cultural History

Alka Pande

with contributions by Johan Mattelaer,
Philip Van Kerrebroeck and Amrita Narayanan

HarperCollins *Publishers* India

Dedication

In praise of Shiva, the Absolute Truth,
and in celebration of *vilas*,
the earthly pleasure that infuses
life with an added lustre.

Contents

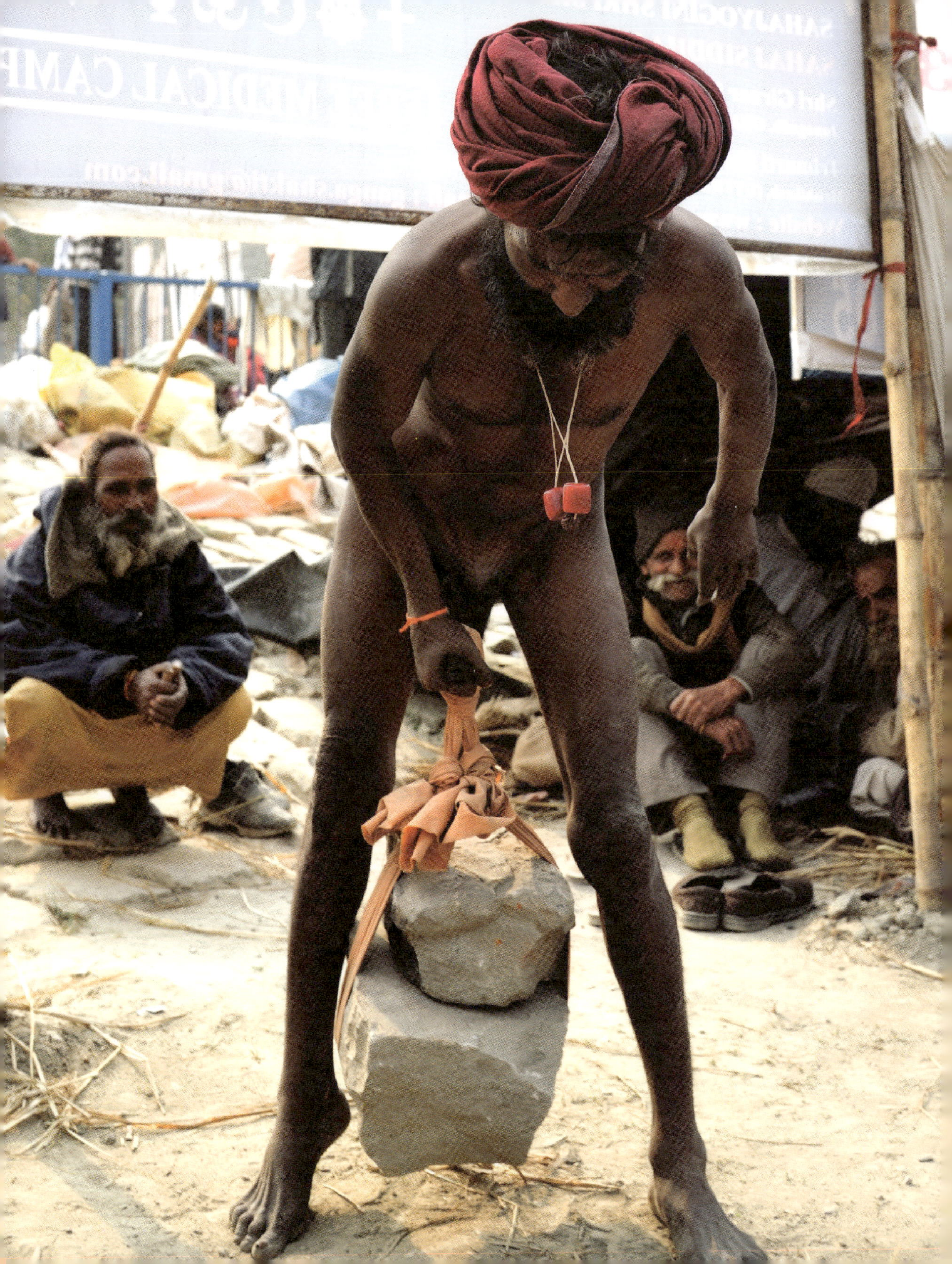

Introduction

Alka Pande

'In this society, the norm of masculinity is phallic aggression. Male sexuality is, by definition, intensely and rigidly phallic. A man's identity is located in his conception of himself as the possessor of a phallus; a man's worth is located in his pride in phallic identity.'

—*Last Days at Hot Slit: The Radical Feminism of Andrea Dworkin*

Stick of joy or pleasure, power or shame, the phallus is an incredible organ invested in the male body. In fact, as Philip Kerrebroeck puts it in his book, *The Human Penis: Organ and Instrument*, 'Phallus' used to indicate a penis that is in a state of erection. Through history the phallus has been the cynosure of all eyes—the male gaze, which could be homoerotic, or homophobic, or the female gaze, which could be an inverted feminist one or the hugely confident gaze of the contemporary empowered woman. The phallus enthralls and interests everyone.

As a woman, writing on the phallus is a hugely challenging task. I am interrogating the phallus in its cultural context, its sacred context, in the context of gender identity and sexuality, and of course in a playful interpretation in popular culture. What is exciting for me at this point in my life is that I am beyond gender, in that wonderful space where I can be masculine one day and feminine the next day—for gender is fixed whereas sexuality is not. I intend to approach the study of the phallus in this book through the lens of shifting sexualities, which is inherent in each one of us.

The erotic

A Naga sadhu at a religious procession in India.

In his essay, 'The Significance of the Phallus', Jacques Lacan differentiates between 'being' and 'having' the phallus. For him, men are considered to 'have' the phallus, while women, who do not have the phallus, are considered to 'be' the phallus. Judith Butler in her discussion of 'The Lesbian Phallus' talks of Freud and the transfer of the meaning of 'phallus' from the penis, the male organ, to other objects of similar anatomy and shape, such as a cigarette or a skyscraper. However, from Butler's perspective a skyscraper better resembles the vagina, the female reproductive organ—thus, for her, it is in femininity that true power resides.

For most heterosexual males, their penis or 'that thing' is the most precious. They start playing with their 'thing' when they are babies in their prams and this goes on till they attain maturity—I often wonder if they are insecure about their organ, touching it to see if it is still there. On the opposite end, most women look at the male organ with wonder and awe. Some men like to say that many women have 'penis envy', while women experience a sense of male aggression through the penis.

The human penis is not only the organ that a man holds in his hand a couple of times everyday to urinate but also the organ of procreation. It is an instrument of pleasure for the man and his partner. From the prehistoric to the present, the human penis, thus, has been a recurring motif in visual culture and religious thoughts of nations and civilizations across the world. As you'll see in the book, in many cultures and societies, the human 'phallus' has been regarded as a symbol of power, veneration and sex.

Every time a man experiences an orgasm the phallus explodes, then dies, then returns to life, time and again. Thus, the term 'phallic resurrection', as coined by the Jungian analyst Eugene Monick. The phallic resurrection cycle is a recurrent cycle of tumescence after detumescence. The pervasive and often extensively crude sexual phallic worship can also be read through this concept. Be it the worship of the rustic Roman God Priapus, who is often symbolized by an enormous penis used as a threat against thieves, or the spiritual lingam, the regenerative maypole, the Herm of Ancient Greeks, or the Egyptian Djed Pillar of Osiris used for resurrection—the phallus has always been endowed with restorative properties.

Erotic statues adorn many ancient buildings and temples in India.

Before I get into a serious narrative of the phallus—the tone, texture, voice and the myths surrounding it—there is also an immersive, seductive, sensual and cultural journey of this part of the human body that has always fascinated many. In different societies, depending on their location and religion, the phallus transforms and gets its own unique cultural identity.

For me, the phallus becomes both an icon of pleasure and procreativity—literally a pleasure stick, the vortex and source of great pleasure during sexual intercourse and the carrier of semen, the seed from which the life-force emanates. The phallus and the vagina come together in sexual intercourse, in which often the phallus, or the lingam, is considered the presiding deity of pleasure; while the dark and cavernous vagina, or yoni, is the holder or receptacle. In Indian culture, the overriding emotion generated as a result of the meeting of the yoni and the lingam is pure orgasmic delight—the French call it 'la petite mort' and Indians call it 'sambhoga ananda'.

The eroticism associated with the phallus can be broken down into distinct layers, depending on the epoch, region or culture. In the eastern parts of the world, particularly India, there is a very clear relation between exoticism and eroticism, where sex is almost similar to a spiritual experience—the pleasure derived from the act of sex transports one to a higher spiritual realm. In ancient India, sexual intercourse was an act of pleasure and not just a device for procreation. Evidence of this can be found in literary texts from that period as well as in architecture. Several temples and monuments, like the ones in Khajuraho, have elaborate depictions of people in various positions of sexual congress. Due to this emphasis on the value of sex transcending procreation, the phallus was revered for its ability to bring pleasure, a tool essential for a man and a woman to come together in the ultimate act of sensual gratification. Despite being the repository of pleasure—in many ways pleasure forms the backbone of human society—the phallus is also a source of power, pleasure and shame at the same time.

Through the power of the phallus comes yet another manifestation of human nature which is seen in the physical assertion of male supremacy, as seen in rapes of women in times of warfare, particularly in medieval and modern India. It was because of the fear of male aggression that the concepts of jauhar and sati became institutionalized in Rajput societies. In modern societies, honour killings also arose due to the fear amongst communities of the exploitation of women's sexuality and vandalization of their character.

Symbolism

Phallic symbolism has been one of the oldest and most prevalent phenomenon in religion, culture, literature and art. The earliest known representations go back to the prehistoric times, apparent in cave paintings and megaliths that are found at several sites across the world. Starting off as a symbol of fertility and virility, the phallus has gone through numerous interpretations through the ages. Though the actual organ itself has always been as important—for men, their phallus has always been an indicator of virility and the ability to father offspring that will carry on the strongest genes, while in male animals, it is used as a means to ward off any rivals, sexual as well as territorial.

This obvious connection between the physical and symbolic ensured the phallus featured heavily in cultures. Though the ways of representation are quite distinct between the East and the West, even though in the western part of the world the erotic symbolism of the phallus is emphasized upon whereas in the eastern part of the world, religious symbolism holds dominance. In ancient times, religion played a vital role in phallic imagery, while in the more modern age art and culture have taken over the space of phallic imagery and interpretation. In pre-modern societies, the penis was a tool of magic, potent charms and fecund rituals—from castration to circumcision, from ornamentation to mutilations. As society started evolving, the cult of the penis underwent transformation as well.

An illustration depicting the erotic from a Kamasutra.

In medieval societies, male patriarchy reigned supreme, and the penis became a tool of both power and shame, with this reaching the zenith during the second-half of the nineteenth century when Victorian prudish attitudes came into being. Michel Foucault commented on this in his trail blazing work, *History of Sexuality*, writing about how notions of male patriarchy came into form against the onset of the undercurrents of female subversive sexuality, like covering piano legs and sandwiches because of how the angles of the piano and the cutoff parts of the sandwiches appeared to resemble the female vulva.

By the advent of modern society, the phallus was taken to another level—it became a symbol of pleasure. Today, the erotic and sexual nature of the phallus has given way to many subcultures that celebrate its sexuality. The modern male became a predator, a man about town, a broad-shouldered, lean-hipped hunter of his own pleasure. At the same time, the penis turned into a dildo—seen as emasculating male power, where new-age feminists rejected and went beyond the male member using a rubber form to simulate the same pleasure earlier only drawn via the penis.

The 'Oscillating Phallus' of the twenty-first century, is it truth or imagination? The new-age urban, literate man of the twenty-first century is comparatively more sexually evolved. Going back to the *Kamasutra* where it was clearly stated that in sexual intercourse the pleasure of the woman was as important as that of a man's, the urbane man takes delight in being a possessor of a phallus which he uses with empathetic inclusion of feminine pleasure. The phallus then becomes a more embracing tool of pleasure rather than a one-sided penetrating stick of joy.

In that sense, the contemporary male is completely a different kettle of fish. Sometimes hunter, sometimes hunted, the new metrosexual man can be androgynous and bisexual with equal flourish. He is dressed elegantly, often in feminine aesthetics; for same-sex orientations are no longer looked at as orientations of the devil and not hunted with draconian cruelty as it was in early modern Western societies.

Religion, culture and the phallus

Religion and phallic imagery have been closely intertwined, a relationship that goes back to thousands of years. During pagan times, forces of nature were the first to be worshipped—one would pray to the elements for protection and survival. Slowly, anthropomorphic beings started replacing the more generic natural elements. These 'gods' had specific attributes and possessed distinct powers to control not only nature but also human desires. Since birth and procreation has always been sacred, gods or deities representing fertility were often depicted with ample and enlarged genitalia. Over the years, the phallus began to be revered on its own and didn't need a deity accompanying it. Several cultures worshipped the phallus due to its life-creating abilities, a practice that involves highly elaborate ritualism. In these cultures, fertility is not just limited to the sexual realm but also means general prosperity and luck. This is extensively discussed in the book later on.

In the Indian context, the phallus took on a different form, one closely associated with religion, spirituality and sexuality, all at the same time—the lingam. Associated with Shiva, the Hindu god of ascetism, eroticism, time, space, destruction, yoga, dance, and the primordial parent with his partner Parvati; in Hindu temples the lingam rests on the yoni, which represents the female aspect, and together they symbolize divine creation. In the Hindu trinity of gods, Brahma, Vishnu and Mahesh (Shiva), with the third regarded as the destroyer of the universe—in this context, destruction leads to regeneration of life. Shiva's lingam represents the creative power of the phallus. The erect position of the lingam suggests that it harbours the power to create life within it, the seed being contained inside and not discharged yet. Through the last thirty years, I have been confronting the phallic image of Shiva right from the 'ardhva lingam' form or the erect phallus in some intriguing images of the 'ardhanari Shiva', where Shiva as the great primordial Indian god symbolized truth, beauty and maleness and appears in the syncretic or androgynous imagery of Siva/Shakti, Purusha/Prakriti. The lingam and Shiva also serve as a reminder of the immense self-control that a yogi, or ascetic, which Shiva is depicted as, possesses. There are thousands of yogis in India that are followers of Shiva and they attempt to gain the same kind of control over their bodies as Shiva through years of meditation. It is considered one of the most important achievements of a yogi when he has complete control over his physical, including sexual, needs. The ability to command one's body supposedly leads to nirvana or salvation. Thus, the phallus, in the form of the lingam, becomes associated with not only sexuality but spirituality.

Ritualism and spirituality related to the phallus is not restricted to India. Several ancient cultures have elaborate ritualistic ceremonies that revere and celebrate it. In Japan, there are festivals dedicated to the phallus, the most noteworthy being Kanamara Matsuri, where a huge milieu of devotees, usually from the Shinto religion, offer their prayers to the phallus in order to bring good fortune into their life. Min, the Egyptian god of fertility and agriculture, was an integral part of important ceremonies like coronations of new pharaohs. Often portrayed with a giant erection and represented in hieroglyphs simply as a phallus, there were quite a few orgiastic rituals associated with him. Min is also referred to as Khnum, the creator of all things and also the Divine Potter, depicted with a potter's wheel through which he created human bodies. The ancient Greeks had gods such as Hermes, Pan and Priapos, who were all related to fertility and most representations of them show large phalluses. Phallophoria, or religious processions dedicated to the phallus were widespread in many cultures. The Greeks were known for their phallic processions as part of Dionysiac celebrations—these were quite hedonistic in nature as opposed to Japan where similar festivals are comparatively sombre.

In ancient Rome, phallic charms were quite prevalent. These had protective purposes and were mostly used to ward off evil spirits. Mutunus Tutunus was a familiar phallic marriage deity, not humanized at all but depicted only as a phallus. It was ceremonial for Roman brides to straddle his phallus to prepare themselves for marital sex. The Native American tribe Hopi worshipped Kokopelli who symbolized fertility, both for reproduction and agriculture. Kokopelli is often depicted as a humpbacked flute player with an exaggerated phallus and is part of Hopi fertility rituals. Phallic imagery was quite prevalent in the Mayan civilization, too. There have been several ancient Mayan sites where phallic architecture has been discovered like in Chichen Itzá and Uxmal. The phalluses are of different varieties and sizes, in some instances attached to a human body or on their own. For the Yucatec Mayan, freestanding monoliths called 'xkeptunich' were very common. Most of these are found in or around temple complexes, signifying their use in religious rituals—the Templo de los Falos, or Temple of the Phallus, in Uxmal is a clear example of this. Uxmal also has phallic-shaped waterspouts as part of the architecture, which draw parallels between the life-giving properties of water and the ability of the penis to create life. Smaller sized portable phalluses are also found at various Mayan sites. These were primarily used as charms or in shamanic rituals. In Africa, too, a number of tribes venerate the phallus—for chieftains and warriors adorn themselves with phallic ornaments symbolizing strength and masculinity. Tribes such as the Yoruba and the Fon had divine spirits called Orisha, Eshu-Elegbara or Legba, trickster gods that preside over sexuality. He is also the messenger that communicates between different realms and is depicted with a large phallus and for Legba, sex is the ultimate connection between two beings. His voracious sexual appetite is quite well-known and priests generally revere him with dances with wooden phalluses that emulate copulation.

The exploration of phallic imagery in the Islamic tradition is quite complex. The phallus is mentioned in quite a few ancient Islamic texts but mostly in the context of shame and morality. Jalal al-Din Rumi, the renowned thirteenth-century Persian mystic, used phallic symbolism in his poetry to describe the inner meanings behind mundane things. 'Masnavi–yi–Ma'navi' is a bawdy and lascivious tale where Rumi uses the icon of the phallus as an esoteric symbol, and thus the concept of phallocentricism becomes the channel of human desires and aspirations. For Rumi, manliness or masculinity was not dependent on the physical object, and by that virtue on the phallus itself. Sexual debauchery was considered similar to moral depravity. There were clear demarcations between the sublime and the vulgar. Meanwhile, in Islamic architecture, several references to phallic imagery can be found. Minarets are quite frequent; tall, erect phallic-shaped structures that tower over the landscape. In a lot of monuments, there is a central dome surrounded by four minarets on different sides, for example, the four minarets at the Hagia Sophia in Istanbul, the Faisal Mosque in Islamabad, and many such historical monuments found all over India which alludes to the feminine being restrained by the masculine. Christianity, too, had an interesting relationship with the phallus, both culturally and spiritually, this is discussed more in the chapters ahead.

Psychology of the phallus

As the understanding and cultural place of the phallus changed, different movements resulted in unique concepts regarding the phallus. These shifts were studied extensively by theorists and psychoanalysts over time. One cannot leave out the psychosexual doctrines of Austrian psychoanalyst Sigmund Freud in this context. Freud's psychoanalytic theories discussed the evolution of the human brain in five distinct stages of sexual development—oral, anal, phallic, latent and genital. For him, understanding sexual development was a key to understanding the psyche of a person and that cognitive behaviour was directly related to stages of sexuality that a person has goes through. The phallus became extremely relevant in this regard. The 'phallic stage' is when one starts to become self-aware of his or her sexual anatomy, a time when one starts to show signs distinct to their sex. Social constructs of gender roles come into play while a person starts falling into the category of a boy or a girl. For men, masculinity becomes synonymous with sexual prowess as their bodies start to change. Freud creates the hypotheses about the Oedipus complex, which is a deeply-connected desire with the parent of the opposite sex. This is considered quite controversial and has been challenged by later psychoanalysts. Other concepts such as 'penis envy', where a female is jealous of a male for possessing a penis leading to a feeling of inadequacy and inferiority, are also integral to Freud's theory of psychosexuality. Later, 'phallic monism', a term proposed by Chasseguet-Smirgel came into being, which describes the possession or not of a penis as being the key factor in one's psychosexual development.

Like Freud, Jacques Derrida had a lot of theories that were focused on the phallus. The idea of 'phallocentricism' found in *Writing and Difference* talked about the fact that most of the history of the world has been documented through a phallic perspective. There are very clear overtones of masculinity and patriarchy in the way western culture is presented through the ages. Phallocentricism is combined with logocentrism, the idea of language being the rudimentary way of representing reality. This hybrid called 'phallogocentrism' can be defined as a masculine voice that influences the language in which events are registered in the history of mankind. For psychoanalyst Jacques Lacan, the original factor of difference within linguistic symbolism is the phallus. Lacan refers time and again to Lévi-Strauss, who used a very structured social world order and Ferdinand de Saussure, who uses the science of symbols to draw conclusions to his interpretation of the symbolism within the phallus. It is the very first divergent in human beings, separating the male from the female. With age, a person forms their individual ego based on the core difference of having a phallus or not.

The modern age and pop culture

The convergence of the cultural and psychological in terms of the phallus results in the translation of the phallus as portrayed in fields such as art and literature. Despite its religious and spiritual place in history, phallic imagery has primarily been used for its sexual and suggestive qualities. Throughout history, there have been many periods of sexual awakening. Important movements such as the Renaissance and Humanism laid emphasis on celebrating the human body and shifting focus from God to Man. Sex began to be talked about, not just as an act of procreation but also one of pleasure. Taking inspiration from the early Greek and Roman civilizations, these movements started drawing parallels between sexual intercourse and the ability to be artistically creative. Several works by the Italian Rennaissance painters like Leonardo Da Vinci in the drawing of the *Vitruvian Man* and Michelangelo in the sculpture of David and the *Fall of the Man*—where they went back to classical Greek representation of muscled bodies, for example in the iconic Rocoon group of the high Greek art—highlight the aestheticism behind the phallus and the human body. A lot of the works also revolved around Graeco-Roman figures, mythological or otherwise. Nude figures were one of the most common subjects in the art produced in this age. The proverbial fig leaf had blown away.

Later, the phallus enjoyed a space of its own in pop culture. The pornography industry has to be mentioned in this context. Although a major portion of pornographic content made is women-centric—men being the target audience—the phallus is represented in several ways, especially taking its size into consideration. In this context the phallus remains a sexual organ but also becomes a tool of dominance. Often it is seen that the borders between pain and pleasure is blurred, both almost blending into each other to create the ultimate sensual experience. At times, it can be caricaturized into something unnatural and distorted but the idea of deriving pleasure always remains at the core. Sex in pornographic videos often reflects the societal gender norms. The man usually in the position of power, possessing the 'stick' to keep the woman in his control, and the woman in a more submissive position, allowing herself to be used in whatever way the man desires. In BDSM (Bondage Discipline Sadism Masochism), the dominant person, be it a man or a woman, always possesses a phallic-shaped object, which is a clear indicator of their superiority over the other.

The phallus has had a separate identity of its own, distinct from the identity of Man. Almost being independent entities, one wonders which of the two is in control of the other. There have been so many movements and studies based on it, all trying to decode the exact functionality and symbolism behind it. From a physical entity, the phallus has moved on to being a cultural emblem of sorts. David M. Friedman's book, *A Mind of Its Own,* is quite descriptive of this in the way it explores the status of the phallus in culture and Man's relationship with it. He goes deep into the details of how this organ has contributed towards shaping mankind throughout history. A very interesting angle introduced by him is that of the penis-enlargement products that have become quite the booming industry in recent times. These products are not just for the sake of impressing or pleasuring the sexual partner, but also to feel more masculine and be satisfied with one's own image. The idea of manhood relates directly to the penis and each individual has his character affected accordingly by it.

The path-breaking and iconic erotic text, the mother of Indian erotic text, the *Kamasutra* dated to anywhere from 2nd CE to 4th CE was first brought to notice in the English-speaking world by the Victorian Indophile Sir Richard Burton who published the *Kamasutra* consisting of 7 books and 36 chapters. The concluding chapters of Book 7 are devoted to aphrodisiacs and recipes for enlarging the penis and the virility of the man associated with the organ.

Pha(bu)llus attempts to bring all the multiple levels of interpretation regarding the phallus together into one comprehensive book. The purpose is to understand the enigma behind phallic representation through the lens of culture, religion, history, art, literature, psychology and many such disciplines. It can be quite complicated, almost impossible in fact, to form a completely singular theory that explains why the phallus is the sensation that it is. One must peel away each onion-like layer before reaching some kind of nucleus. This book is not just an interdisciplinary one but also explores significant timelines that depict the evolution of phallic symbolism. The various ways in which the phallus has been considered relevant, even though quite distinct from each other, come together to contribute in the constantly transforming notion of the phallus. Most of these are interrelated. One has to know that none of these interpretations can exist in vacuum. In quite subtle ways, or at times direct, each has an impact on the other.

This book is an attempt to interrogate and reflect upon the phallus and it's potent depiction in art thought, literature, philosophy and cultural symbolism . In a way it is a compendium of multivocal interpretations of the phallus. Thinking along this global, cosmopolitan trajectory which for me begins with the erect phallus of the primoridial God Shiva moving into a diverse landscape of ideas across time space and ideologies. I thought of my two Belgian friends and collaborators of an iconic *Kamasutra* exhibition which I had curated in the city of love, i.e. Paris at the Pinacothèque, in the winter of 2014. The two brilliant Belgian urologists who had been collecting phalluses across continents for more than four decades and writing, exploring and even treating them medically. What better way to enrich the book with inputs from enlightened scholars, medical practitioners who had both a cultural and medical understanding of the penis. Johan Mattelaer has written extensively on the subject in European and Far Eastern culture, Philip Van Kerrebroeck a practicing urologist and an educationist scholar, hones his understanding of the phallus through his vast collection of phalluses, particularly from primitive cultures in Africa and South America. Psychoanalysis has always been very important for me in the understanding of cultural icons so choice and inclusion of the third author Amrita Narayanan, a practising psychoanalyst and clinical psychologist, furthers our understanding of the phallus through the readings from contemporary psychoanalysis, was ideal. Amrita is a woman who has analysed the understanding of the phallus, sexuality, and desire through the tracings and readings of modern psychoanalysts...For me her inclusion also brought in the right gender balance to the book.

It is this very diversity of thought, the multivocality of voices which will bring in a tour de force to the understanding, interpretation and cultural value of the phallus in contemporary societies and thought. Each of these scholars contributes with a point of view which is imperative to learn more about these multiple perspectives in order to fully comprehend the significance of phallic symbolism. The difference in perspective in eastern and western cultures also plays an important role in this regard. This juxtaposition presents newer angles in the evolution of the phallus, as an individual cultural entity.

In the end, *Pha(bu)llus* is an exploration of this intricate network of ideas and beliefs regarding the phallus, digging a little deeper into what is perhaps the most recognized cultural motif in the history of the human race.

THE PHALLUS ACROSS EASTERN ASIA

Johan Mattelaer

Bhutan

Nam gawa the wei woe lu yoe;
phung dang si yang they nang yoe.

Fun and pleasure are located below the navel;
the dispute and trouble are also located there.

—Bhutanese proverb

Ladakh, Zanskar, the Spiti Valley, Nepal, Mustang, Tibet, Sikkim, Bhutan and Arunachal Pradesh were, and in some aspects still are, small kingdoms with the same identity—Mahayana Buddhism also known as Lamaism, or Buddhism of the large prayer wheels. Buddhism in these kingdoms was grafted on the old, primitive religions of the region. These old religions were animistic in nature and deified rocks, trees, rivers and mountains. In Tibet, this was the Bon religion—the many-coloured prayer flags and the heaps of stones called chorts, which are placed as offerings on mountain passes originated from the Bon religion. The same blue prayer flags can be found in Mongolia, where the sacred piles of stones are called ovoos. For Buddhists in the Himalayas, the phallus is still a symbol of protection and fertility, as it was in the primitive religion of these countries.

In Bhutan, there are many festivals that celebrate phallic culture. Phallic rituals with animistic background originated in central and eastern Bhutan. In early fifteenth century, the phallus could be seen on walls, hanging from roofs and used as a talisman. Lama Drukpa Kunley used the phallic symbolism to spark new ways of thinking among people he encountered. The Divine Madman was trained as a monk in Tibet but left to become a nomadic teacher of Buddhism, travelling through the western half of Bhutan. He understood that the easiest path to enlightenment was through surprise and humour. Through the constant use of his 'magic thunderbolt', Kunley would shock people away

Symbolic teacups with male and female genitalia are gifted to the bride and groom on a wedding (above), while painted phalluses can be found all over Bhutan (left).

Phallic symbols and shapes are found all over Bhutan. At religious festivities, clownish figures or atsaras (bottom, left) are present with a wooden phallus to amuse the people with bawdy jokes.

from life distractions and they would understand the futile nature of wants and instead, seek enlightenment. Kunley was known for his ability to strike down the demonesses of Bhutan with his 'thunderbolt', and this sparked the Bhutanese belief that the phallus can ward off evil spirits and transform them into protective deities. In the Divine Madman's anecdotes, the phallus represents protection and subjugation while also acting as a way to promote fertility. Drukpa Kunley was not ashamed to use his own phallus and sexual excitement, that he called 'the thunderbolt of flaming wisdom', to bring women back to the right path of faith by terrifying and expelling the female demons. 'The Saint of 5,000 women', as Kunley was sometimes called, knocked and bound the female demons in order to change them by a holy game of love in good spirits. Even today the holiest of sanctuaries is devoted to Drukpa Kunley, like the Chimi Lhakhang temple near Punakha.

Devotees adorn their houses with phallic paintings and children and domestic animals wear phallic talismans to enjoy protection from demons or other hostile spirits. Here we see a comparison and analogy with the phallus in the Roman empire although there was no direct influence nor contact. Huge phalluses are painted on the façade when the gomchen or wandering monk consecrates the new house. These phalluses painted on the houses protect the occupants. This is due to the three deities the painting symbolizes: Vhana Doirje (the root of the penis), Jambeyang (the middle part) and Chenresi (the glans). These three deities extract the evil from heaven, the interspace and the earth.

During festivals, 'atsara' or clowns perform by carrying a phallus and are present to relax the crowd. Such display attempts to explain the naked truth of our own lives, how we tend to hide what is natural.

Phallic images clearly have an aggressive significance in Bhutanese culture. At the entrances to the traditional fortified monasteries or dzongs, gatekeepers or dvarapalas can be seen in the shape of male warriors, their power incarnated in the phallus as a living symbol. Phallic art permeates the Himalayan religion

and is a source of great pride—even in the temples deities are represented with a phallus. At weddings, men and women drink from wooden teacups with symbolic genitals to promote fertility and sexual happiness.

Phallic worship is also found in Tibet. Here also, the phallus has an unequivocally protective character without any trace of the obscene or any erotic significance. As an illustration of this, phalluses are found in nunneries in Ladakh and also in Arunachal Pradesh.

Dvarapalas, or gatekeepers, are found on monasteries; their power embodied in their penis.

Thailand

God sleeps in a stone, breathes in plants, dreams in animals and wakes in man.

—An old Asiatic saying

In Thailand, phallic amulets play an important role in everyone's daily life. Each amulet represents the powers derived from the specialist who made it, the material it is made of, the formulas engraved on it and the consecration ceremony. These protective amulets are an example of a popular belief which grew out of elements of Buddhism, Brahmanism (Hinduism) and animism. Thai people believe in magic and supernatural powers, and in their ability to give protection from sickness and evil. A phallic amulet is only regarded as authentic if a recognized specialist or bonze, as they are also known, has handed it over in person.

The phallic amulet was introduced in the fifteenth century, when Thai monks began to hang phallic symbols on the belts of the smallest and weakest amongst them. According to beliefs at that time, the boy, whose childish penis is still entirely covered by the foreskin, represents the unprotected one. The grown man, on the other hand, whose bell-end constitutes the tip of the erect member, symbolizes fortification and strength. It was, therefore, in monasteries that they began to give boys phallic amulets to offer them some protection. The idea appealed to other social classes and what was once discreetly used as a protective tool in the isolation of monasteries was now found all over Thailand.

Two types of phallic amulets are found in Thailand: dôkmai cao, or flower genius, a large and usually crudely carved phallus out of wood or stone; and the palat khik, or honorable surrogate penis, which is a smaller amulet.

Phalluses are found at many Thai temples, like these at Chao Mae Tuptim shrine in the centre of Bangkok.

The dôkmai cao is dedicated to the female spirits of nature and placed in temples along riverbanks and beside the sea. In the capital city of Bangkok, many boys and girls can be seen honouring Mae Thap Thim, the goddess of the Banyan tree, who

Phallus shapes are used extensively in charms of various kinds. Palat khiks are fertility amulets, sometimes worn as a belt by women (top, right).

Animals are popular motifs in amulets. Like this palat khik, which has a monkey carved—monkeys symbolise dexterity and linguistic skill.

like Shiva is presented as a lingam under the shadow of a banyan tree. All kinds of offerings are brought to the shrine, and the bearers of these gifts all beseech the goddess to bless them with children and to meet the person with whom they are to have these children. Sometimes, these shrines are very similar to Hindu lingams. In or around some temples, we can see a large number of dôkmai cao, as at the Chao Mae Tubtim shrine where literally hundreds of penises (phalluses), some made from small wooden carvings to big stone sculptures, stand ten feet tall and are decorated with ribbons making this shrine quite unique. It honours Chao Mae Tubtim, a female fertility spirit. Women visit this shrine when they are trying to conceive, leaving offerings of lotus and jasmine. Some dôkmai cao are smaller and are put on an altar in the house, or in shops or smaller chapels.

Palat khik means 'accompanying sex'; khik is a vulgar word for penis in Thailand. These make the wearer invincible, especially in the sense of protecting him from being pierced by a knife or a spear. They are also known to protect young boys from being bitten by snakes or dogs.

Palat khiks for adults are inscribed with magic formulas. The most common is kan ha nêha, or the heart of the killer, which is a formula which wards off all dangers and illnesses. According to popular belief, a palat khik should be worn on the stomach if the wearer is going to fight, on his back if he is going to try and escape, on his right if he wants to influence important people and on his left side to seduce a woman. To cure a fever, a palat khik should be soaked in alcohol and the alcohol given to the patient to drink.

A big dôkmai cao in the garden behind Wat Pho temple (top, left), and a phallus surrounded by four Buddhist monks at the Wat of Wae Hon Son.

These amulets are made of all kinds of materials—the most valuable are made of coral or ivory. Sometimes, a tiger—a symbol of strength and invincibility—is depicted. In addition, sometimes tiger's teeth, claws and tattoos are also worn as an amulet to frighten evil spirits. Some palat khiks have legs and tails, representing the lizard, which ensures that love is everlasting in the wearer's life and that all difficulties may be overcome. Phallic amulets with a monkey are also very popular—the monkey, or ling lom, stands for dexterity and linguistic skill. He also represents Hanuman, the monkey god from the Hindu epic, *Ramayana*.

Many of these palat khiks bear a female figure embracing the phallus. These are, above all, fertility amulets, since they often bear the inscription: 'human beings are always engendered by the genitals of the father and the mother.

Vietnam and Cambodia

Lingams are phallic symbols, basically, and the flow of the river over them sanctifies the water.

—A description of a visit to the Kbal Spean river near Angkor Wat

Among indigenous communities in Vietnam, like the Joraï, large tombs are built in commemoration of the dead. A collective tomb would contain as many as thirty wooden bodies. These hand-cut wooden figures represent humans with significant sexual attitudes and pregnant woman, also regarded as symbols of fertility.

In the course of their long history together, Vietnam and Cambodia have always been rivals but both countries have been influenced by Hinduism and the cult of the lingam. For centuries, the Cham kingdom in Central Vietnam and the Khmer kingdom in Cambodia fought each other.

A collective tomb from the Jörai people in the province of Gia Lai, Vietnam. The numerous hand-cut wooden statues represent humans with significant sexual attitudes and pregnant woman.

Vietnamese Cham art can be divided into two broad periods. Up till the tenth century, Cham art was strongly influenced by the art of Indonesia (Java), where Hinduism was the dominant religion and hence it was strikingly emotional and expressive. Between the tenth century and the end of the fourteenth century, Cham art declined as a result of the long wars with the Vietnamese kingdoms in the North and the Khmer in Cambodia. Cham art also became more formalistic in this period. A number of examples of lingams dating from this period can still be seen today in My Son and in the Cham museum in Da Nang. Perhaps one of the greatest examples of the lingam in Cambodia can be seen at Angkor Wat, a temple complex and the largest religious monument in the world. Angkor Wat was

These two lingams, which date back to the pre-Khmer period, are the Mukhalinga, Nui Ba The, An Giang, 6th–7th century AD (top, left), and another that dates back to 9th–10th century (top, right). Two stone lingams at the archaeological site of My Son, Vietnam (below).

originally constructed as a Hindu temple dedicated to the Hindu god Vishnu for and by the kings of Khmer Empire—it gradually transformed into a Buddhist temple towards the end of the twelfth century. The famous temples were built between the ninth and the thirteenth century. Consequently, the sculptures and art at Angkor Wat reflect the changing religions of the kings, which shifted from a Hinduism that focussed on Shiva as the central godhead to a Hindu religion with Vishnu as the central figure, followed by the conversion to Mahayana Buddhism with Avalokiteśvara or Padmapani, a bodhisattva who embodies the compassion of all Buddhas. This is why we find such magnificent lingams in temples in and around Angkor Wat, resting on the female yoni.

A very interesting place near the temples of Angkor Wat is Kbal Speam, where the water from the mountains flows down to the fertile fields around Angkor Wat. The clear water runs over thousands of phallic lingams in order to stimulate the fertility of the fields.

During the reign of the Khmer Empire, young girls were isolated during their first menstruation and entrusted to the priests. This period was called Tcol meulap or 'entry in the shadow'. This tradition is documented by Chou Ta-Kouan, or Zhou Daguan (1266–1346), a Chinese diplomat under Temür Khan, the emperor Chengzong of Yuan, Ta-Kouan writes: 'At the age of 7 to 9 years for the wealthy girls and at the age of 11 years for the destitute they ask a Buddhist or Taoist priest to deflower them. They call it Tchen-t'-an. Each year the authorities chose a day that corresponds to the fourth Chinese moon and let it know to the whole country. That day, when the night comes, is the time for Tchen-t'-an. The priest himself may approach only one girl.' During his trip in 1413 to Cambodia, the Chinese traveller Ma Huan (1380–1460) narrates that the future bride is first deflowered by the priest and can only join her husband and family for the wedding feast in company of the priest and her parents. The deflowering would be done using a vaginal dilator or a hymenal dilator, like this one that dates back to the sixteenth century.

A sixteenth-century bronze deflorator from the Khmer period (above).

China, Mongolia and South Korea

In an effort to appease the spirit of a young woman, the villagers erected several gigantic penis sculptures on the beach.

—From the Korean legend of Auebawi and Haesindang

According to Confucius, there was only chaos in the beginning. Heaven and earth existed together and were not separated. There were two forces or principles: the male and the female. Confucius named them 'yang' and 'yin'. These principles separated gradually. Yang ascended to create heaven and yin descended to create earth. Nature was the result of the unification of heaven and earth—the male and the female. This way all plants, animals and everything in heaven and earth was created. Heaven was father, and the earth mother. In this way, yang became the phallus and yin his female counterpart.

Although in China, phallic worship probably existed also in connection with fertility, today very little of it has survived. Over time, a rather comprehensive and refined erotica culture came about, which can't be interpreted as phallic. In Chinese literature, the penis and the phallus are rather poetically named 'jade stalk' especially in reference to sex.

Today, most phallic archeological findings are conserved in museums where daily utensils like big spoons with obvious phallic handles dating to the sixth century are found. In Yunnan, an axe with the head of a deer and a phallic end was found, while a beautiful copper shovel with an anatomical phallic from the Dian kingdom (208–206 BC) has been excavated.

A large phallic stone found near Karakorum, the first capital of Mongolia founded by Genghis Khan. The stone points towards a fold in the green hills of the steppe, which symbolizes female genitals.

Big phallic structures are found all over South Korea, like these dol hareubangs which are large guard megaliths carved from basalt (p.42), and these large phalluses carved in the local rock stone at the Palgongsan national park.

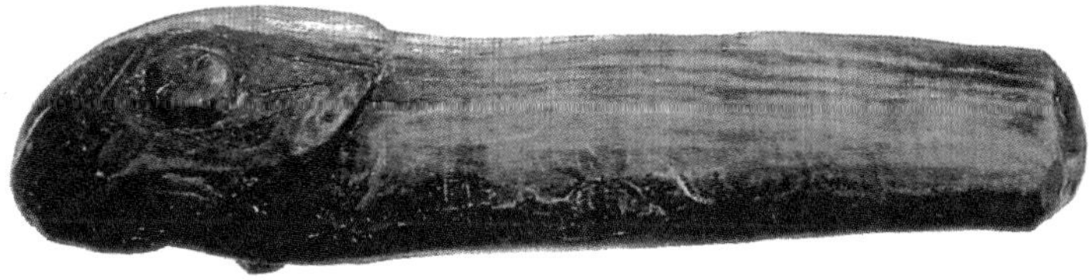

Wooden phallus found in the Anap-chi pond, dating back to the Silla period, around eighth century AD

Near Karakorum in Mongolia, the previous capital of Genghis Khan, there is a big phallic stone, the Kharkhorin Rock, pointed to a grove in surrounding green hills, which symbolize the female genital. In the drylands of Mongolia, an 11-inch long obsidian phallus was excavated. In the Kyongju National Museum of South Korea, a beautiful wooden phallus from Silla can be found.

From the same period, phalluses on clay figures and vessels which were seen as a symbol for a good harvest and fertility are found. In Korea, phalluses on rock paintings dating back to the Bronze Age have also been discovered.

On the island of Jeju, on the southern tip of South Korea, Dol hareubangs, also called tol harubangs, hareubangs, or harubangs, are large guard megaliths, carved from basalt, which can tower up to 3m. These megaliths were considered to be gods offering both protection and fertility and were placed outside the gates for protection against demons travelling between realities. These statues were first built by Kim Mong–gyu in 1754 at the gates of the Jeju Fortress. After the three gates were torn down, two were moved to Gwandeokjeong, while two more were relocated to the entrance of Samseong temple. These anthropomorphic phallic statues wear a mushroom-like hat and are always grinning with big bulging eyes. Their hands rest on their bellies like they are enjoying a private joke, with one hand slightly higher than the other. The name of these statues is made from the Korean word for stone, dol, and the Jeju dialect word for grandfather or senior, hareubang.

The Palgongsan Mountain is considered the center of Buddhist culture in Korea. Treasured not only for its natural beauty, the mountain also hides within its folds a number of old temples and historic sites from the Silla Dynasty (57 BC–935 AD) and a field of phalluses carved in natural local rocks.

Indonesia

The temple of Prambanam on the island of Java, Indonesia, is surrounded with an array of phallus-shaped statues, just like this large lingam stone (below). Other sites like Candi Sukah have erotic statues like this man grasping his phallus with infibulation around the penis (left).

The Lingga is a naturalistic rendering of a huge phallus with four balls below the tip. These balls may represent the first set of four peaks that surround Mount Meru.

—Ann R. Kinney, *Worshipping Siva and Buddha*

Although we can find phallic cults among the many indigenous people one finds in a large number of islands that make up Indonesia, the lingam culture entered the main island Java when Hinduism was introduced in the Medang kingdom in central Java at the beginning of the eighth century.

Medang's religion centred on the Hindu god Shiva, and the kingdom produced some of Java's earliest Hindu temples on the Dieng Plateau. Around the ninth century, the Sailendra dynasty rose in Kedu Plain and became the patron of Mahayana Buddhism. These ancient kingdoms built monuments such as the well-known ninth-century Borobudur and Prambanan in central Java. The temple of Prambanam is surrounded with an array of phallus-shaped statues and inside the temple exists a big stone lingam.

Around the tenth century, the centre of power shifted from central to eastern Java. The eastern Javanese kingdoms of Kediri, Singhasari and Majapahit were mainly dependent on rice agriculture, yet also pursued trade within the Indonesian archipelago, and with China and India. The Javanese kingdom of Majapahit was established by Wijaya and by the end of the reign of Hayam Wuruk and with the coming of Islam to Indonesia, the Majapahit kingdom and by consequence Hinduism, went into decline and Islam became the dominant religion in Java at the end of the sixteenth century.

In a private collection, we found an old big stone lingam, about 120cm in height, in Eastern Java, which dates back to before 1500 AD. At the top there are inscriptions written in a highly decorative script, called Kadiri Quadrate characters, that was usually reserved for concise monumentalized inscriptions. Unfortunately, most of the characters can no longer be deciphered.

The Candi Sukuh, a Hindu temple located in Central Java, has a distinctive thematic relief from other temples where life before birth and sexual education are the main theme. This monument is a simple pyramid structure with reliefs and statues in front of it, including three tortoises with flattened shells and a male figure grasping his penis. A giant lingam with four balls, about 1.82 metres high, made in 1437, representing penile infibulation was one of the statues found here. The realistic phallus with four balls under the tip represents the four mountains around the mythological Mount Meru. H.N. Sieburg decrypted in 1841 the text on the phallic sculpture as: '... initiation of the holy Ganggusudhi in .... The symbol of masculinity is the essence of the world. On the Saturday of Wuku Watyang.'

The most folkloric remain of Hinduism in Java today is the puppet show known as Wajang Kulit. This is the Indian story of the Ramayana represented by a shadow puppetry in the local language with popular expressions. As also seen in the festivals in Bhutan where clownish figures appear, in Wajang Kulit, one of the puppets named Semar, a phallic figure, accompanied by his sons, plays a comic role to relax and amuse the people.

Hinduism still persists on the island of Bali. Although the Balinese pantheon has many gods, they believe only in the divine entity, Sanhyang Widi Wasa, the dominant spiritual spirit together with Brahma, Vishnu and Shiva. Since Shiva is worshipped in Bali, we can find many lingams in the temples.

Little wooden figures with an enormous phallus, known as meummedi, are found all over the island and believed to bring good luck and drive away the

Erotic figures like these dot the landscape of Candi Sukuh in Java, Indonesia.

evil spirits. In Sanur, life-size phallic straw men are set up to guard over the rice fields and to protect fertility—these beliefs come from the indigenous culture and are disappearing today. In Lombok, indigenous people offer puppets with distinct genitalia as a wedding gift to stimulate fertility.

On the island of Bali, little wooden figures with enormous phalluses, known locally as meummedi, are believed to bring good luck (left, top right). Similarly, in Lombok, indigenous people offer puppets with prominent genitalia as a wedding gift (top, left).

Japan

Erotic expression in Japan is graphic rather than plastic, and secular rather than religious. This is the exact contrary of the case in India.

—Theodore Bowie

In 1896, W.G. Aston, the pioneer of West European research into the long-hidden secrets of Japanese culture, made reference to the fertility cults that existed throughout Japan at that time, even though their prevalence was diminishing under the pressure created by the country's rapid modernization and increasing European influences.

'All travellers in Japan, especially before the Revolution of 1868, must have observed numerous evidences of a phallic cult. The Government have of recent years done their best to suppress this very gross form of nature worship, but it still exists in out-of-the-way places... I once witnessed a phallic procession in a town some miles north of Tokyo. A phallus several feet high, and painted a bright vermillion colour, was being carried on a sort of bier by a crowd of shouting, laughing coolies with flushed faces, who zig-zagged along with sudden rushes from one side of the street to the other. It was a veritable Bacchic rout.'

Figures like these in Dosojin at Karuizawa Nagaro Prefecture are common around the town of Matsumoto. The stones are always rounded, and depict a man and a woman, sometimes holding hands.

These fertility cults are believed to date back to ancient times and were inspired by rock formations in suggestive shapes, known as the 'yin-yang' stones (inyo-seki). One of the earliest manifestations are the so-called, dosijin or gods of the way, where images of a couple in an intimate embrace are drawn on a phallic form or rock, representing, 'wagojin' or the gods of harmony. The stones are usually rounded off and are particularly common in the region around Matsumo. These gods are supposed to protect passing travellers.

In Japan, phallicism is not the worship of a sexual organ, but a glorification of life through the medium of this organ. According to Genchi Kato, the earliest reference

A woodcut drawing showing women shop for harigata or dildos.

to phallicism was an ancient document dating back to 807 AD, known as *Kogoshui.* The text tells a story where in a fit of rage, the rice god Motishi-no-Kami sent a plague of locusts to destroy the rice harvest. The people then offered up a phallus to appease him and thereafter it became customary to make an offering to the god every spring in the form of a phallic figure carved in wood or ivory.

Since Japan, in contrast to China, was not influenced by Confucianism, it is a country that has always been open towards sex and sexuality. The worship of both the male and female genitalia, whether to encourage fertility or to ward off the evil eye, has been a constant feature of traditional Japanese folk religion since ancient times. These beliefs were later carried over into Shintoism and Buddhism, where sexual union was regarded as an illustration of the cosmic principle. Shintoism, which presupposes an intimate relationship between nature and man, is what gives Japanese eroticism its special power.

The relation between religion and sexual symbols is already expressed in the Japanese legend about the creation of the world. The legend goes that after

Izanagi and Izanami had planted the giant phallus—which they received from their ancestors—in the belly of the earth, they use it like a spear to descend to the earth themselves. The spear is then transformed into the tree of life and both dance circling the tree. At the end of the dance, Izanagi and Izanami come together and imitate the story of the creation—Izagani is the spear and Izanami the lump of earth which was opened up by the magical power of the spear. In this way, the two make love and create many other islands. After bearing many offsprings, Izanami gives birth to the fire god—as a consequence her womb is destroyed by the flames and she dies.

The link between a sexual god and a certain place is indicated most by forms of images standing beside a road of a field. These objects are valued because of the protection they offer against evil or epidemics and the assurance of agricultural fertility that they may provide. The larger sites involve increasingly elaborate buildings where the enshrined gods address a form of fertility that is more specifically human, adding to prayers for bountiful harvests, the conception of children, safe childbirth, easy delivery, cures for sexually-transmitted diseases or the desire to find a partner.

The first phallic object in Japanese history is found on a 'hantwa', clay figures placed within the large earthen tombs called kofun from the third century onwards. The ancestors of the present imperial line were buried in these kofun and an important characteristic of the grace goods found within them was the presence of hantwa, which may have had a protective role after death. An excavation in Gunma Prefecture shows a male figure with an erect penis. This was the first time in Japanese history that an apparent phallic symbol can be firmly identified as a representation of the male sexual organ.

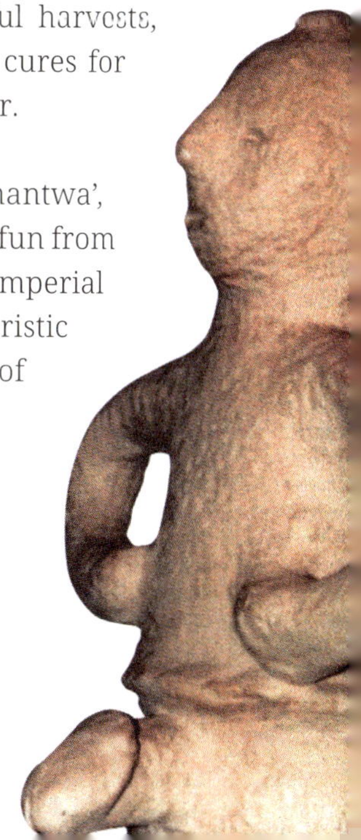

From the third century onwards it was common practice to bury ancestors of the imperial line with hantwa or clay figures, like this one found in Gunma Prefecture.

Indeed, when we inspect daily life in Japan closely, it is evident how the phallus is really integrated and

In the upper social classes of the Samurai, it was customary to give shunga artworks and prints that had erotic drawings and depictions as a wedding present.

男女色交合之縁

A Japanese shunga print by Utagawa Kuniyoshi from the book Hyakki yagyō *dating back to 1825.*

associated to in Japanese culture. In an account dating back to 1864 by Sinclair Coghill, a Victorian traveller to Japan, it was found:

'The male symbol was the only object of veneration, apparently; in various sizes, sometimes quite colossal, more or less faithfully modelled from nature, it held the sole place of honour on the altars in the principal hall and subsidiary chapels of the temple. Before each, the fair devotees might be seen fervently addressing their petitions and laying upright on the altar, already thickly studded with similar oblations, a votive phallus, whether of plain or wrought cut wood from the surrounding grove or of other more elaborately prepared materials.'

Most Japanese erotic drawings, known as shunga art, were made between 1600 and 1850 and are woodprints of Ukiyo-e. Ukiyo-e literally means pictures of the floating world. This period reflects the shift in economic power from the imperial court to the town and the declining influence of the Samurai, as a result of the up-and-coming merchant class. These artistic prints are erotic works which combine great delicacy of line with the brutal realism of sexuality and have little to do with phallic culture as such.

Outside the world of shunga, in the ancient rites of pre-Buddhism, the phallus or 'heavenly root', as Rawson calls it, is venerated as a holy object. In temples, large and small, votive offerings in the form of phalluses are made. Naked figures with enormous phalluses were offered in village chapels to protect people from catastrophes like famine, earthquakes and sickness. In Shinto religion, the phallus was also a symbol of solar energy.

Even today, people evoke the supernatural power of the phallus by wearing little phallic amulets to give them strength and ward off sickness.

In Japan, one of the most well-known fertility festivals, or honenmatsuri, is the Tashiro Jinga festival in Nagoya, where a huge wooden phallus is carried in a procession through the streets and rice fields. At the end of the procession, the wooden phallus is thrust into a vagina made of straw, while sake (rice wine) is poured over their union. A traditional phallus festival is also held in Kawasali in the month of April. In another festival, celebrated in March, it is customary to set fire to a gigantic wooden phallus, and when the flames are leaping all around it, it is plunged into the sea. In Nishio-shi, as part of the Shinto harvest celebration, or at Tenteko Matsuri, at the end of March each year, a 2.5m-long phallus is carried through the streets while women with smaller phalluses in their hands lead the way.

These festivals are a prayer for progeny and potency. Though today, these festivals have become more commercial and mainly attract tourists, within many temples we can still find these original phallic sculptures being worshipped. According to the legend, if a woman visits a shrine and strokes one of the wooden phalluses, it greatly increase her chances of finding a husband.

Another example of the phallus being integrated culturally is the netsuke. The netsuke is a small, delicate toggle, usually carved in ivory, which was attached to the sash or to the cord of a purse hung from the sash of a traditional Japanese costume. Some netsukes developed into very fine examples of Japanese erotic art, while some, which are mushroom-shaped, very obviously represent the phallus—in Japanese, the phallus is also referred to as matsutake, with means mushroom.

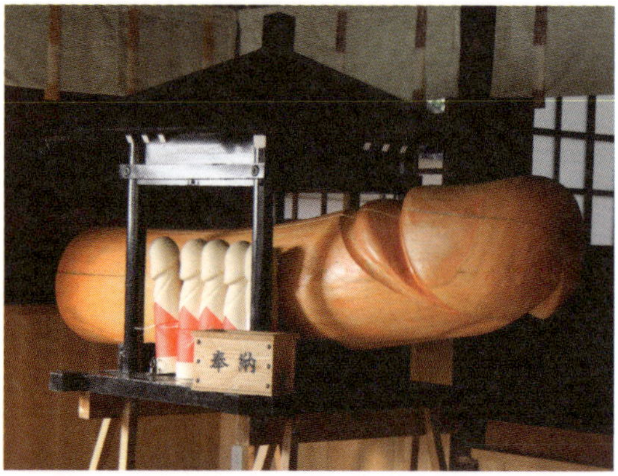

Phalluses are worshipped all over Japan. During Hōnen Matsuri. or the Harvest Festival, a large wooden phallus is carried from a shrine called Shinmei Sha (in even-numbered years) or from Kumano-sha shrine (in odd-numbered years) to a shrine called Tagata Jinja. Phalluses can be found displayed at temples across the country.

There are incidences of dildo–phalluses in Japanese culture too. In older times, when an imperial officer left on a long journey, he left a carved phallus behind for his wife, as a dildo, made of various materials like wood, ivory, stone, tortoiseshell or horn. These dildo-phalluses are called 'harigata'. The idea was that the wife could make use of the object during her husband's absence, instead of taking a lover and tainting the honour of the family. In time, ivory became the most popular material for harigatas, as also for netsukes. As their popularity rose, sculptors gave their imagination free rein—phalluses would have landscapes and erotic scenes delicately carved between the pronounced veins which figured on it.

Another example of the importance of the phallus in Japanese culture is the occurrence of enormous phalluses, often of gigantic dimensions, that are used in the phallic contests or trials of strength, known as yōbutsu kurabe, depicted in Japanese shunga art. This was not a new phenomenon. Enormous phalluses had been depicted before in Japanese art, and even during the Middle Ages, contests between men with huge penises had been portrayed.

According to Akiko Yano, who divided these phallic contests into three different categories, there may be some connection with the prehistoric phallic stones of the Jomon period (10000–300 BC). He also pointed out that there were two medieval works of Japanese literature—*Shin sarugaku ki* and *Tettsui den*, both described by Fujiwara no Akihira that make reference to a large penis:

'His phallus is said to be as thick as a beam and curved like a rainbow. The glans is huge, as if wearing a woven hat. Its length is eight sun (about 24 cm) and the width is about four fingers. The veins look like a crawling spider. It is as strong as a tree stump and as hard as an iron hammer. It wakes up during the night and only relaxes at dawn. Therefore, there were no women who dared to marry him.'

The oldest image of a phallic contest is to be found on a medieval handscroll in paper, known as *Mitsui Kachi-e emaki*, painted by Abbot Kakuyù of Toba,

There are many kinds of netsuke, like this woman on a phallus and this one carved in the shape of a mushroom, which signifies the phallus.

on which two themes are depicted: the first being the phallic contest and the second a farting battle. The first shows naked men with surrealistically huge male members. The second shows priests and other men 'fighting' each other with anal wind. There are no women and no sexual elements in the scenes. The *Mitsui* is probably a faithful copy of two even earlier manuscripts.

During the shunga period, prints of this kind gradually became more erotic and many original handscrolls from earlier periods were copied in the new artistic style, including the phallic contests. The words used to describe the contest—kachi-e—came to mean 'images of victory', even though there was no sign of a victor in any of the prints. All that can be seen in most of them are naked men, who allow their gigantic penises to be measured in a kind of non-sexual competition.

The exaggerated and comic depiction of the male genitalia in the kachi-e therefore formed the basis for the portrayal of the male body in the erotic shunga prints, whose artists adapted this iconography to their own style, particularly during the Edo period. The enthusiasm of these artists to make copies of the phallic contests of an earlier age has given them an important position in the history of Japanese art. Consequently, we must conclude that the depiction of phallic contests was an original and fruitful idea in the history of the Japanese iconography of the body—from the medieval times till the end of the Meiji period (1886–1912)—and should not be regarded as frivolous, ridiculous or vulgar.

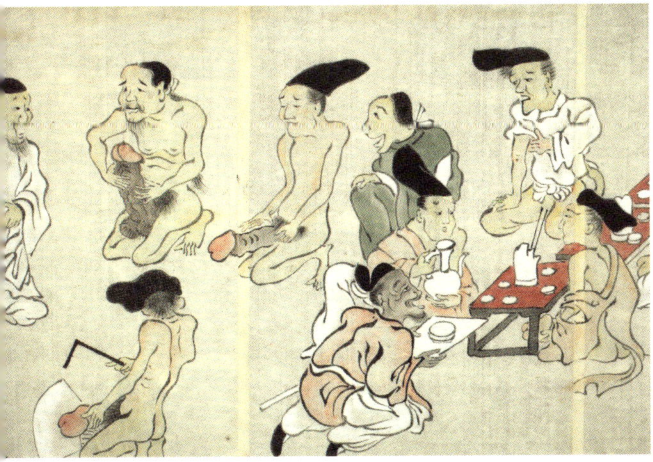

Phallic contests were popular throughout Japan; like this nineteenth-century illustrated scene showing yobutsu-kurabe (phallic contest) by Toba Satoru, (top, left), and this handscroll showing yobutsu-kurabe (phallic contest) with individual competition.

With roots in nearly all primitive cultures and ancestral beliefs, and influenced by devotion to the lingam as seen in Hindu culture, the cult of phallus has spread all over eastern Asia, from the Himalayas to Japan. Even today we see phallic sculptures worshipped in many temples and ceremonies.

WORSHIP OF THE PHALLUS IN INDIGENOUS SOCIETIES

Philip Van Kerrebroeck

A man from the Big Namba tribe with his traditional penis cover.

Statue of Saint Vigor, a French saint, with a pronounced phallus hidden inside his back.

Traditionally, an indigenous society or an indigenous ethnic group refers to a group of people who identify with each other based on similarities such as common ancestry, language, society, culture or nation. Individuals are often bound together through different aspects such as an inherited status and history; a shared cultural heritage, ancestry, origin myth, history, homeland, language or dialect; symbolic systems such as religion, mythology and ritual, cuisine, dressing style, art, and even physical appearance.

Ethnicity is often used synonymously with ambiguous terms such as nation or people. In the English language, ethnic or ethnicity can also have the connotation of something exotic, related to cultures of more recent immigrants in an area already established by a founding population. In many societies the number of people who comprise an indigenous group may vary in number—the Han Chinese being the largest—while the smallest groups are limited to a few dozen individuals like numerous indigenous peoples worldwide.

The religious context of colonial development often influenced the observation of certain aspects of indigenous societies, especially the interpretation of rituals related to phallic imagery. Therefore, early descriptions of phallic customs and rituals are not always reliable and often aim at finding a confirmation of primitive aspects of indigenous societies. In general, ethnic or tribal art is considered as the visual arts and material culture of indigenous peoples, and is still also known, although controversially, as primitive art. Nowadays, the term 'primitive' is criticized as being Eurocentric and pejorative. Indeed, the term primitive is not fair as many examples of tribal art are far from being primitive, neither in form nor in meaning. Recent research which is based on persisting oral tradition and sometimes archaeological evidence allows for a better interpretation of the role and significance of phallic depictions and their use in indigenous societies. Moreover, there is ample evidence that so-called 'western' societies have used phallic imagery in the course of their existence. However later, it was the Victorian aspect of western societies that vigorously tried to eradicate phallic references, and even tried to hide any documentation

The interior of a nineteenth-century ethnographic museum collection in Europe (left) and a cabinet with a collection of Roman votive phalluses (right).

related to the subject for the general public. Hence the 'secret cabinets' in many European museums.

Historically, tribal arts have been collected by western anthropologists, private collectors, and museums, particularly ethnographic and natural history museums. Initially, collecting examples of tribal art has been inspired by the Western myth of the 'Noble Savage', and lack of cultural context has been a challenge with the Western mainstream public's perception of tribal arts. In the nineteenth century, non-Western art was not seen by mainstream art professionals as being art at all.

In recent years though, perception of tribal art is becoming less paternalistic, as indigenous and non-indigenous advocates have struggled for a more objective scholarship of tribal art. Before Post-Modernism emerged in the 1960s, art critics approached tribal arts from a purely formalist approach, that is, responding only to the visual elements of the work and disregarding historical context, symbolism, or the artist's intention. This is especially true for phallic objects and even more for blunt phallic representations. Hence these objects were often not preserved but destroyed or secluded in 'secret' cabinets. In time however, some brave individuals came to see the importance of these remnants of often sophisticated rites and saved them for conservation. Still, many objects with clear sexual aspects, were hardly visible for the general public and often were only accessible with special permission, based on specific research questions.

Phallus-shaped objects have been used since prehistoric times—like this stone phallus from New-Guinea.

In recent years, a more open approach to sexual matters has increased the interest in the phallus and its representation, as well as among scholars and researchers. Private initiatives, for example museums, have specifically focused on erotic art and dedicated expositions to such art, lowering the threshold for public and academic interest. These initiatives have shown that phallic representations have been used all over the world and across cultures, and in many parts of the world still continue to be used as art forms and expressions of culture. Unfortunately, despite more research showing the complex significance and the role of the phallus, many phallic objects remain, quoting the poet John Keats, only 'things of beauty', but nevertheless 'a joy for ever!' In order to appreciate the beauty and understand the importance and role of phallic objects, it is useful to study their place in the framework of tribal art in general, the ceremonial and religious nature of such art, the subject and craftsmanship of these artefacts, and the specific visual and symbolic language they employ.

Africa

Usually, the term 'African art' does not always include the art of the North African parts along the Mediterranean coast, as these areas had long been part of different traditions. Although art from Egypt and North Sudan can be included in African art, the cultural artefacts coming from these geographic areas are so different that often they are clubbed under the umbrella of Egyptian art. Additionally, artistic artefacts from the Coptic culture in Egypt are still very distinct from other creations in Egypt. Furthermore, North African art contained Islamic art for more than a millennium. The art of Ethiopia, with a long Christian tradition, is also different from that of most of Africa where traditional African religion was dominant, until relatively recently. Therefore, African art can be divided into Ancient art (pre-historic and pharaonic), Muslim art of North and West Africa, the Christian art of East Africa and the ritualistic art of these and other regions.

A Nok terracotta figure (above) and African men with elaborate markings (left).

African art, in general, describes the historical and modern (often non-tribal) paintings, sculptures, installations and other visual culture from native or indigenous Africans and the African continent. The definition may also include the art of the native African and African diasporas such as African American, Caribbean, and other American art. Despite this diversity, there are some unifying artistic themes when considering the totality of the visual culture from the continent of Africa, with sexuality, masculinity and fertility being common themes. African art contains masquerade, metalwork, sculpture, architecture, and fibre art. Phallic thematic can be found in every type of African art and is executed in many materials.

Most African sculptures were historically in wood and other natural materials that have not survived from earlier than, at most, a few centuries ago. However, much older terracotta figures and objects can be found in a number of areas. They are representative of African prehistoric art and indicate that thousands of years ago a phallic culture was present through Africa.

There is a vast variety of styles, often varying within the same context of origin depending on the use of the object, with wide regional trends apparent.

A group of wooden phalluses from the Fon Benin (above). P.73, left to right: a Waga sculpture, a Sidamo phallic stele, a Bura stone and terracotta phallic grave pole, and a Djenne phallic stopper.

Sculptures, including three-dimensional phallic objects, are most common among groups settled in the areas drained by the Niger and Congo rivers in West Africa. There are many direct images of deities, often with a prominent phallus, and also masks made for religious ceremonies with phallic symbols. These African masks had an important influence on European Modernist art, inspired by their lack of concern for naturalistic depiction and uninhibited expression of sexually-linked aspects.

Since prehistoric times, the phallus or its symbolic image—in erected or non-erected state—is very prominently present on the African continent. This phallic imagery can be a form of material representation of the penis, as encountered in daily life but also as an element used in many different specific and sometimes complex rituals. The cultural context of phallic representations in Egypt was quite obvious; their phallic imaginary was rather acceptable as it was explained by sophisticated religious practices.

From the beginning of the exploration of black Africa by non-black people, many myths developed regarding penis size among black people. Several of these 'phallic fantasies' are still cultivated and reproduced. Though there is no epidemiological data that indicates that the average black penis is bigger than in any other race, there is ample anthropological evidence that in some African tribes, the average penile length within that tribe is largely above the general mean. Hence, the white colonials were apparently impressed, probably by comparison with their own penis, and stimulated the myth of the 'big black cock' (BBC). This raised an interest in phallic representations as basically encountered in the whole of black Africa, and this also stimulated research into their meaning. Furthermore, the often quite impressive and exaggerated size of

phallic representations in Africa undoubtedly were an extra-stimulating factor for this perception. As a consequence, early publications tried to accentuate mainly the sexual connotations of these images, and used this to confirm the brutal and primitive nature of these indigenous populations.

Phallic images in Africa can be present in public spaces as well as in sacred environments like temples and places of worship, in private houses and family altars. Some phalluses may be permanently displayed, but others are only used during specific ceremonies, which follow strict customs and rules.

Some indigenous populations in Africa use individual body decorations in order to enhance manhood and impress females. A typical example of this are the Borana men, who live on either side of the southern Ethiopian and northern Kenyan border. The Borana men wear a 'phallic' kallaacha on their forehead. The kallaacha is made of cast aluminium, ivory or bone, and is worn during the tribe's initiation and age-grade ceremonies. The Konso people, who are from south-western Ethiopia, are also famously known for their Waga sculptures, which are unique carvings made to celebrate and pay tribute to deceased men who hit significant and memorable milestones in their lives, such as killing an enemy or a wild animal. Beside a prominent phallus, these sculptures are complemented with a sculpted kallaacha on the front, indicating the importance of this supplementary macho symbol. Furthermore, in Sidamo, a province in the southern part of Ethiopia, the Sidama tribe erect stone phallic steles, some found dating back to 1200–1700 AD. These structures are believed to be connected to burial rites, though research has shown no skeletal remains. Interestingly, similar stone sculptures have been found in the Bura culture from Niger.

(Clockwise, upper left to right): an Ibo mask from Nigeria surmounted with phalluses, a Fon voodoo altar from Benin with phallic objects, a Borana chief from Ethiopia with a phallic kallaacha and a wooden Nguadi phallus from the DR Congo.

One of the oldest indigenous groups of Africa were the Nok, an early Iron Age population whose material remains are named after the village of Nok, situated in the Kaduna State in Nigeria. The Nok culture appeared in northern Nigeria around 1500 BC but vanished under unknown circumstances around 500 AD. Their famous terracotta sculptures were first discovered in 1928 and some have an obvious exaggerated or erected phallus.

Similar figurative sculptures in terracotta with phallic references have been found in the Inland Niger Delta dating back to the eleventh and seventeenth centuries, a period marked by the successive trans-Saharan trading empires of Ghana, Mali and Songhai in West Africa. Within the Bura area (a set of archaeological sites in the lower Niger River valley of Niger and Burkina Faso), several terracotta grave posts from the Iron Age civilization have been found, which clearly present an exaggerated phallic form. As the majority of these works emerged via the art market during the 1970s and 1980s, little is known about their original context, their functions or the exact tribes that produced them. It is known that some of the phallic structures were connected to graves of male individuals and hence they probably indicate a male burial site. Nevertheless, some phallic objects were obviously intended for daily use, indicating that these representations were considered 'normal', even outside a specific gender or sexual context. As fertility and procreation have always been an important element of ritual activities, it is not remarkable that many ritual objects present with phallic forms. However, the exact significance and specific use of these phallic figures remains enigmatic.

There is a long and bloody history of the West's fascination with the African penis, and European colonialists disseminated accounts of African men's allegedly outsized penises. These accounts were alternately taken to be evidence of their greater natural sensuality or their closer proximity to animals. Even now, some African tribes are still famous for their penis enlargement or penis elongation techniques. The Batammariba, a tribe found in Togo and Benin, is known for ancient penis-enlargement techniques. They

(Clockwise, bottom left onwards): A Lobi stool with phallic handle from Burkina Faso; a Makonde giraffe bone votive with phallus and vulva from Tanzania; a Makonde phallus from Tanzania; Dagari male wooden figure from Burkina Faso; Makonde male and female wooden votives, a Masai horn medicinal pipe from Kenya and a Songye ritual spoon from the DR Congo.

practice these techniques during male initiation ceremonies into adulthood where traditional herbs are pounded and rubbed on the penis to achieve penile enlargement. The Karamojong tribe from north-eastern Uganda has also been known to employ penile stretching techniques. From early youth, men of this tribe hang ever-increasing numbers of circular stone disks from the end of their penises, and over the course of a number of years they can achieve impressive penile lengths. By the time a young boy has reached his teenage years, he may carry up to 10kg on his penis, which by this time can measure to about 45cm or more in length. To avoid sitting on the elongated appendage, the men will often tie their penises into knots and tuck them away. When they sit on the hand stool they carry around with them, their penis touches the ground, often drawing lines on the soil in response to the movement.

A phallic ornament known as pikuran worn by Kirdi women in Cameroon.

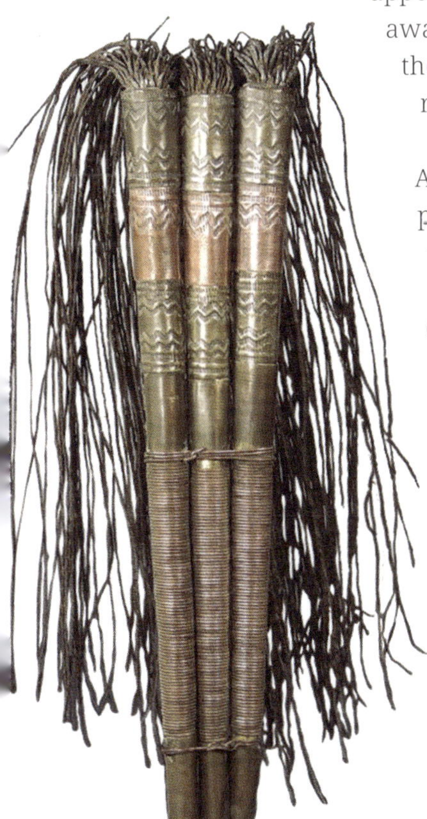

Ancient Malians, particularly the royals of Djenne, decorated their palaces with phallus-like piers and columns at the entrance of their palaces and decorated the walls with phallus motifs. Similar features can be seen on the pillars of many temples across Africa, often interpreted by western scholars to be phallic symbols, but may often be more subtle and subject to varying interpretations. Like the ancient Egyptian pharaohs, Ethiopia's Aksumite kings built temples with phallic pillars in ancient cities such as Konsu and Axum, and monolithic pillars with phallic representation have also been discovered in Madagascar.

In Central Africa, the image of the phallus is omnipresent and represented in various forms and materials. Numerous wooden phalluses were sculpted by the Fon from Benin with a great variation in size. Some of these wooden phalluses were used during dances in which, sometimes, women bind the phallus on their pubes and at other times planted them in the ground as a symbol of male power.

Penis elongation techniques are common amongst African tribes. In the Karamojong tribe from Uganda, penis elongation is done by hanging discs from an early age.

But a phallus can also be found in objects for daily use, such as headrests and little stools. Different tribes from Zaire (the former Belgian Congo) created very powerful phallic images amongst them. The Makonde used phallic images in secret rituals related to masculinity and fertility. Elegant ritual objects with phallic symbols can be found amongst the Lega. Even the medicine man used a special spoon with phallic end to deliver a magic potion in order to enhance potency. The use of phallic objects by the medicine man or witch doctor in the framework of healing sessions is quite common amongst different tribes.

The phallus is also used to indicate the chief's power and decorates his sceptre. In Central African tribes, the phallus often represented the male element confronting the female counterpart. The common human form, hence, is sometimes transformed into a phallic figure with additional elements indicating both sexes. In other representations, the male figure is represented as a phallus on two legs incorporating the human and the phallic form in one sculpture.

(Right, top to bottom): the powerful ankh symbol, stone carving with ejaculating penises and Min, the god of fertility with an erect phallus at the Karnak temple.

Gender play is also an intrinsic element of many African tribes. A very particular example is found among the Kapsiki. The women from the tribe wear a 'pikuran', a phallus-shaped ornament made of copper and brass. Like

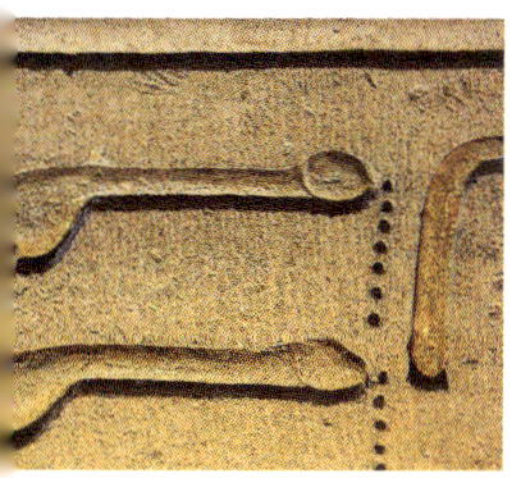

many forms of cache-sex, the pikuran is worn to draw the men's eyes to the pubic area. The different styles of the pikuran denote age, status and certain conditions such as the onset of puberty, marriage and widowhood, as well as tribal origin.

Ancient Egypt

In Ancient Egyptian religion, the penis played an important role, especially in the cult of Osiris. The story goes that Osiris is the ancient Egyptian god of fertility and is depicted as a green-skinned deity with a pharaoh's beard, partially mummy-wrapped at the legs. When Osiris' body was cut in fourteen pieces, his brother, Seth, scattered them all over Egypt. But Osiris' wife, Isis, retrieved all the parts except one—his penis, which was swallowed by a fish. Supposedly, Isis made a wooden replacement in order to conceive Horus, and hence Osiris is sometimes depicted with an obviously erect penis. As a consequence, a wooden phallus would be offered as a separate entity during complex fertility rites in the temple. Some of these have been preserved well. In addition, the hieroglyph for fertility is also represented as an ejaculating phallus.

For the Ancient Egyptians, the phallus was a symbol of fertility, and therefore several Gods and ordinary human figures were depicted as ithyphallic (human form with an enlarged penis). In the early dynasties, phallic amulets can be found, often made of precious stone, with the form of an erected penis, carved or shaped from natural materials represented prosperity, fertility and health. During later dynasties, the image of the male genitals—the penis and scrotum—had spread in use as an amulet made of glazed ceramic or even gold.

The human penis was considered such an important element of the body that the penis of the pharaohs and other important individuals received a special treatment during the process of embalming. Most of the time, the penis was wrapped separately from the testicles and the rest of the body, an indication of the importance of the organ.

Several examples of phallic objects, amulets and representations from Ancient Egypt.

A penis sheath was an essential element of men's costume. A strategically placed strip of cloth was worn to protect, what was considered a vital and sacred organ from environmental elements, working hazards, as well as troublesome insects and tropical diseases. In ancient Egypt, all men adopted a costume that emphasized the genital area, as the penis was regarded as sacred because of its central role in procreation. Some ancient Egyptian drawings depict men naked, except for a belt around the waist from which hangs a strip of cloth forming a penis sheath. During the New Kingdom (1500–750 BC), Egyptian military recruits donned a uniform consisting of a short kilt or merely a penis sheath.

The penis sheath may also have inspired one of ancient Egypt's most enduring icons, the 'ankh' hieroglyph which means 'life'. Some Egyptologists speculate that the ankh sign may have a connection to the ceremonial penis sheath worn by the Egyptian king during the 'heb sed'—a ceremony performed every thirty years after the coronation of the king, where he performed a ritual run-and-dance aimed at proving he was still physically able to rule.

Phallic symbolism was already prevalent in the architecture of ancient Babylonia, representing the phallus of the masculine earth. The Ancient Egyptians developed this to the obelisk that had several functions, both as a reference to the cult of the sun and of the phallus, as a sign of fertility and power.

During the Ptolemaic era, the influence of Roman phallic culture increased the number of phallic symbols used in Egypt. Images of gods related to fertility were 'romanized' and presented as, for example, Priapus with an erected phallus. Beautiful, colourful amulets were widespread and used as offering or simply worn on clothing. Mummies from that time often have phallic amulets attached to the linen bundles that cover the body. Even in the Christian Coptic community small phallic amulets were used, probably more as a protection than as a fertility symbol.

The Arab Peninsula

The Arabs were so much attached to the idea of the superiority of big penises that they conquered the Ottoman Turks, partially due to their ideas about phallic superiority of the Turks. In medieval Arabic literature, the size of the penis is an important subject, so much so that one of the Arabian Nights tales is called 'Ali with the Large Member'. Very discreet but beautiful phallic amulets are documented as originating from the Arab peninsula, probably worn hidden under daily clothes as private protective medium.

The Bible, too, alludes to the size of the penis—as a quote from Ezekiel 23:18–20 said: 'When she carried on her whoring so openly and flaunted her nakedness, I turned in disgust from her, as I had turned in disgust from her sister. Yet she increased her whoring, remembering the days of her youth, when she played the whore in the land of Egypt and lusted after her lovers there, whose members were like those of donkeys, and whose issue was like that of horses.'

A foot scraper with a phallic end from Afghanistan and a carneole phallus amulet from the Arabian Peninsula (bottom, right).

North and South America

Visual arts by the indigenous people of the Americas encompass the visual artistic traditions from ancient times to the present. These include works from South America, Mesoamerica including the Caribbean area, North America including Greenland, as well as Siberian Yup'ik peoples who have great cultural overlap with the Native Alaskan Yup'iks. Pre-Columbian art thrived throughout the Americas from around 13,000 BC to the European conquests. Many pre-Columbian cultures did not have writing systems, so visual art expressed cosmologies, world views, religion, and philosophy of these cultures, and served as mnemonic devices.

Phallic objects or symbols from North America are rather rare and if present, often are very subtle. However, quite many original examples have survived and represent unique iconography and symbolism.

Pre-Columbian penile and/or sexual representations are not very numerous, as many may have been lost after Christianization of the Americas. Nevertheless, existing depictions are diverse in nature and meaning. In general, phallic representations in pre-Columbian Central and South America are versatile and their meaning is multiple. Phallic objects seemed to have had a very important role in daily life as well as in civil and religious ceremonies, and therefore represent an extremely interesting aspect of life in these areas before European colonization took place.

A Chancay wooden figure (left), a stone phallus from Oregon and a Hohokam stone phallus (right).

NORTH AMERICA

Some indigenous tribes of North America (the North American Indians) used phallic symbols in their rituals, although the total number of ancient finds is rather limited. Some early examples found in river beds represent incidentally phallic-shaped stones that were adapted to enhance the phallic form. These sacred objects were kept in a secret place and probably could only be seen by the male members of the tribe. While many of these phallic objects have been lost as offerings in the rivers, it is believed that some of them were incorporated in daily life, like where a phallic form is incorporated in a pipe.

Phallic kachina dolls made by the Hopi Indians are more recent examples of phallic objects from this region. The phallic form in these kachinas is often more discrete, but sexual connotations can still be seen. These phallic kachinas were used by the shaman in rites related to fertility and sexuality.

The Inuit, the indigenous peoples inhabiting the Arctic regions of Greenland, Canada and Alaska, have a particular way of using a functional phallic image. The males use a urination device with phallic ending, made of walrus bone, in order to facilitate urine evacuation without wetting their protective clothing by elongating their penis. The Inuit also make very nice 'oosiks'—made of the fossilized penis bone (or baculum) of walruses, seals, sea lions, and polar bears, which are used as handles for knives and other tools. Sometimes the oosik is polished and embellished with a sculpted human face in polished animal bone.

(Clockwise, left to right): An Inuit oosik and a urination device from Greenland, a Native American phallic stone pipe from USA and a Hopi kachina doll from USA.

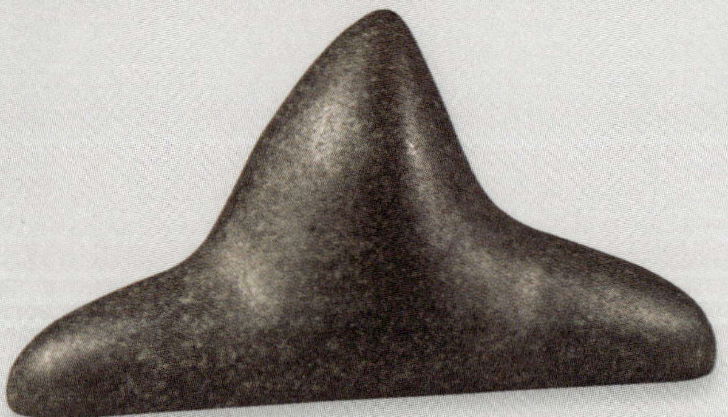

(Clockwise, top left to right): a phallic Kuna nucha figure from Panama, a Vicus vessel with a double phallus, a Nazca vessel with a phallic couple and a Mochica vessel in the form of a man holding his penis, all three from Peru and a Taino zemi from the Dominican Republic.

Central America

Among the Taíno people of the Caribbean, the 'zemi' or 'cemi' was a very popular sculptural object. The zemi stands for a deity or ancestral spirit and is believed to house a spirit. The simplest and earliest recognized zemis were roughly carved objects in the form of an isosceles triangle (three-pointed zemis) and can be seen as primitive phallic representations that have the power to alter circumstances and social relations. Possession of the zemi by Taíno leaders was a sign of their privileged relations with the supernatural world. Important Taíno people living on Hispaniola owned one or more zemis. The zemis represented not the power of the person who owned them, but allies that the person could consult and venerate. In this way, zemis provided contact for the Tainos with the spiritual world.

In Panama, the so-called 'nucha' figures are very popular in the traditional culture of the Kuna people. Some of these nuchas are connected to fertility rites and as such can have a phallic form. A nucha is a healing figure made out of balsa wood and is used by the shaman. The spirit of a living person is summoned in the healing process for soul retrieval and to restore the balance of health to an afflicted individual. The process is accompanied by a shaman's healing chant and the burning of cacao beans in a clay sensor underneath the patient's hammock.

South America

All over South America a rich phallic culture is present. Figures of Kokopelli and Itzamna (the Mayan tonsured maize god) in pre-Columbian America often present phallic content. Additionally, over forty large monolithic sculptures (Xkeptunich) have been documented from Terminal Classic Mayan sites, with the majority of examples occurring in the Puuc region of Yucatán. Uxmal has the largest collection with eleven sculptures. The largest sculpture was recorded at Almuchil measuring more than 320cm high with a diameter at the base of the shaft measuring 44cm.

Three terracotta phalluses from Costa Rica.

Some populations are particularly well-known for their extensive erotic imagery, including very explicit representations of the phallus. The Moche, a population that flourished in northern Peru, have produced numerous ceramic objects depicting humans and animals in a wide variety of sexual acts. These ceramic vessels present free-standing three-dimensional figures on top or as part of the vessel. As well as being works of art, these sex-themed vessels are also functional clay pots, with hollow chambers for holding liquids, and a spout, typically in the form of a phallus, for pouring. Amongst the Vicus from Peru, phallic vessels were used in rituals, as well as amongst the Nazca. From the Chancay population, also from Peru, many wooden figures have been recovered and some of them incorporate a separate phallus that is attached to the body in erect position.

Other populations in different areas, like the Tairona from Colombia, have also produced quite explicit phallic objects. Often their exact role or significance is not known as no written records exist, but it can be suspected that these objects played a role in rites related to sexuality and fertility. Sometimes the image of the phallus is combined with female elements, as is the case of some ceramics by the Calima, also from Colombia. In the Tumaco culture from Ecuador, images of the phallus were widespread based on the numerous examples that have been found. Most of these phalluses were part of larger sculptures, but no intact copies have been discovered yet. However, some impressive self-standing phalluses have survived that probably were individual offerings.

In South America, many ritual objects apparently contained phallic depictions. Well-known for their phallic images are the so called ‘vomitors’, that were used to provoke vomiting after ingestion of hallucinogenic substances.

(Clockwise, left to right): A votive terracotta phallus from Costa Rica, a terracotta Taironas ceremonial phallic knife from Colombia, two terracotta phalluses from Costa Rica, a bone vomitor with phallic end from Ecuador and a Calima phallic figure with indication of a vulva from Colombia (center).

A guesquell of mule hair from Patagonia (top) and a guesquell as applied on the base of the penis (bottom).

Easter Island, that is now a part of Chile, is culturally more connected to Oceanic cultures. A typical object of the original Pasquan society is the ritual paddle, or rapa. These paddles were made out of the local toromiro wood, and have a small but obvious phallus at the lower end. Little is known about this type of ritual paddles, and the double-sided form is unique to Polynesia since they typically have only one blade. Used as part of a pair in seated ritual dances, possibly connected to fertility and to funerary rituals, the paddle is characterized by the abstract carving of an anthropomorphic figure, decorated with a phallus, confirming the relation with fertility rites.

In Patagonia, men would apply a ring of mule hair on their penis before intromission in order to enhance the pleasure for the woman during intercourse. Until the sixteenth century, men in the Topinama tribe in Brazil would provoke poisonous snakes to bite their penises. This caused pain that would last for about six months, but was also believed to significantly increase the size of the penis. At the end of the six months duration, the men had a monstrous-sized penis that delighted their women.

Some South American cultures actually hung heavy, carved jade and other hard stone ornaments from piercings through the skin of their penis and scrotum—these were usually of a temporary ritualistic nature. While some tribes, especially in the Amazon area, used phallocrypts to cover their penis.

A rapa, or a ceremonial paddle, from Easter Island with phallic decoration at the bottom.

Oceania

Oceanic or Oceanian art comprises the creative works made by the native people of the Pacific Islands and Australia, including areas as far apart as Hawaii and Easter Island. Specifically, it comprises the works of two groups of people who settled in the area though during two different periods. They would in time, however, come to interact and together reach even more remote islands. The area is often broken down into four separate regions: Polynesia, Micronesia, Australasia and Melanesia. The former two share a common ancestral culture of the Lapita, while the latter two comprise settlers of the first wave of people into the area. All the regions in later times would be greatly affected by Western influence and colonization. In more recent times, the people of Oceania have found a greater appreciation of their region's artistic heritage.

The artistic creations of these people varies greatly throughout the culture and regions. The subject matter typically carries themes of fertility or the supernatural. Therefore, it is not surprising that phallic objects or objects with phallic elements are widespread and commonly present. Art such as masks were used in religious ceremonies or social rituals, where fertility and masculinity played an important role. Petroglyphs, tattooing, painting, wood carving, stone carving and textile work are other common art forms. Contemporary Pacific art is alive and well, encompassing traditional styles, symbols and materials, but now imagined in a diversity of contemporary forms, revealing the complexity of geographic, cultural and individual interaction and history.

Aboriginal Australia

The indigenous Australians (Aboriginals) are known for performing subincision, a form of body modification consisting of a urethrotomy, in which the underside of the penis is incised and the urethra slit open lengthwise, from the urethral meatus toward the base. The slit can be of varying lengths. This practice is widespread in the traditional cultures of indigenous Australians and is well-documented among the peoples of the central desert such as the Arrernte and Luritja. A subincised penis is thought to resemble a vulva, and the bleeding is

Warriors of the Dani tribe.

A Ramu river boat mound with a phallic top from New Guinea (extreme left) and an Aboriginal pubic cover called Lonka Lonka from Australia.

likened to menstruation. Some stone representations of a phallus with incisions seem to indicate that subincision or other forms of incisions of the penile skin were an important part of their sophisticated rites.

Among some Aboriginal tribes of Western Australia there was a tradition of wearing an ornate, carved pearl shell penile cover, called a 'Lonka Lonka'. It is hung from the genitals by a twisted thong made of human hair. They are often ornately engraved with mainly geometric patterns and the grooves were coloured with reddish ochre.

New Guinea and other Oceanic islands

The phallic representations among the native inhabitants of some ethnic groups in New Guinea vary from discrete to very prominent in form. In the Sepik area, several tribes decorate daily objects like canoe mounts with a phallic image. Additionally, there are also individual phallus sculptures that were used in specific rituals related to the reaching of adulthood and fertility. Little is known about these secret practices as oral transmission failed to document the specific use of these remarkable objects.

(Left to right) A Dani man with his koteka or penis sheath and a Yali man with his genital cover, both from Irian Jaya, Indonesia.

However, the area and its people are especially known for the rich variation in penile covers or penis sheaths, the 'koteka'. The koteka is a phallocrypt, normally made from a dried out gourd, *Lagenaria siceraria*. The koteka is held in place by a small loop of fibre attached to the base of the koteka and placed around the scrotum. There is a secondary loop placed around the chest or abdomen and attached to the main body of the koteka. Men choose kotekas similar to ones worn by other men in their cultural group. For example, Yali men favour a long, thin koteka, which helps hold up the multiple rattan hoops worn around their waist. Men from Tiom wear a double gourd held up with a strip of cloth and use the space between the two gourds for carrying small items such as money and tobacco. The koteka is a traditional form of clothing best known in the Grand Baliem Valley of Western New Guinea and the Ok Tedi and Telefomin regions of Papua New Guinea. It is worn without other clothing, tied in upward position. It is commonly assumed that there is a sexual display element to wearing the koteka. However, according to the locals, kotekas are worn only to cover themselves.

(Clockwise, left to right): a Sepik wooden phallic ritual object; a prehistoric stone phallus, both from New Guinea; a stone pounder with phallic handle from the Marquesas Islands and a wooden healing object with phallic ending from Fiji.

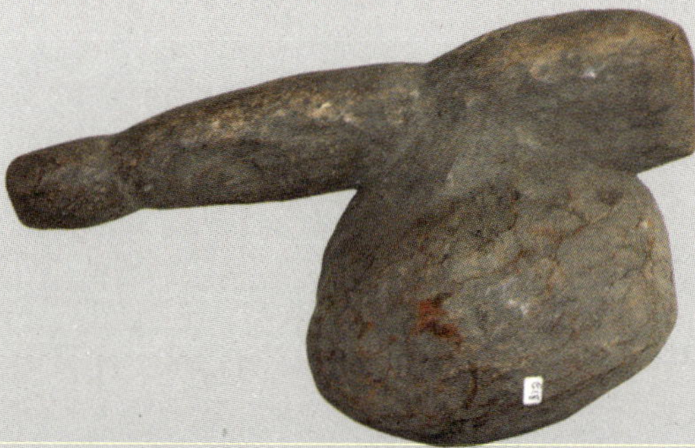

In other parts of the Oceanic continent, phallic representations have been documented less. Nevertheless, some remarkable objects have been preserved. For example, on the Fiji Islands healing instruments with a phallic ending were used in order to promote fertility and sexual performance. On the Marquesas, an island in French Polynesia, pounders used to grind grains sometimes have a clearly phallic handle. It is not clear whether this is just decorative or if a deeper meaning can be attributed.

THE PHALLUS IN PSYCHOANALYSIS: DEFINITIONS, FANTASIES AND THE ROLE OF GEOGRAPHY

Amrita Narayanan

The phallus is not a penis. A penis is a bodily reality, but a phallus is a symbolic construction common to many civilizations and cultures. As a body part, a penis may be alternately hard and soft, full and empty, but as a figurative representation of fullness, the phallus is permanently engorged. The symbol of the phallus commands a power in the human imagination far in excess of the reality of a penis.

To explore the human fixation with the symbolic power of the phallus, I use principles from the field of study known as psychoanalysis. Psychoanalysis plumbs the human imagination for unconscious meanings and fantasies underlying human thoughts and behaviour. Arguing that human beings' interest in pleasure and fulfillment goes far beyond what is possible in reality, psychoanalysts are interested in how humans unconsciously use fantasy to supplement reality. Contemporary psychoanalysis associates the phallus with fantasies of wholeness,[1] completion,[2] power[3] and self-sufficiency.[4]

Every fantasy, psychoanalysis, tells us, covers up a reality. As an emblem of wholeness, the phallus provides an imaginary relief from the inherent lack and incompleteness of the human condition and the impossibility of total fulfillment[5] within a human life.

As a symbol, the phallus is universal and timeless in nature—it has traversed time and geography. It appears worldwide in ancient art, jewellery and tribal cultural ritual, and it features in individual fantasies shared on the couch in the twenty-first-century psychoanalytic clinic. What role does regional geography and culture play in what the phallus promises? How has the field of psychoanalysis been both complicit and insightful in the process of fusing and separating the penis and the phallus? How have particular groups in history and geography—the Sambia of New Guinea and the Dorians of ancient Greece—gone about imagining the phallus? This essay explores these questions to understand how the symbol of the phallus has gained power.

Against Lack: definitions of the phallus from different psychoanalytic geographies

Like other works of art and imagination, the phallus provides relief for the human awareness of lack and transience: the phallus' attractiveness lies in the fact that its visual fullness contradicts a world that is so often empty. The phallus commands a power higher than that of usual art objects. It has become a symbol through human emotional investment. The phallus gets its power from the human wish to avoid feelings of emptiness or lack.

As a field, psychoanalysis has developed differently in various geographic regions of the world, in concert with local geography and culture. While psychoanalysis worldwide agrees that the phallus symbolizes a wishful fullness that negates an essential lack in the human experience, it is worth looking at how this figures in different geographical regions of psychoanalysis. To see the development of the figurative phallus across cultures gives a sense of its diversity, and demonstrates the cross-cultural effect that has transformed the image of a body part (that of the penis) into a symbol (that of the phallus).

A reading of the history of psychoanalysis yields two popular definitions of the phallus—from Sigmund Freud and Jacques Lacan (1901–81) —both geographically located in Europe. In addition, there are two more psychoanalytic notions of the phallus, both with a solid basis in their own terroir and with a far longer history: the exhibitionistic phallus posited by Italian psychoanalyst Carlo Bonomi draws its origins from the phallic worship of ancient Rome, and the bisexual phallus suggested by the Indian psychoanalyst Sudhir Kakar,[6] originates from the worship of the lingam in India . Each of these understandings of the phallus offer a fantasy compensation for the human experience of lack, and approaches the question of whether the phallus is to be associated with the physical body (iconic) or kept abstract (anaiconic).[7]

Freud's concept of phallic narcisism is the first appearance of the phallus in psychoanalysis. The phallus came into Freud's theories via his descriptions of how a boy's and a man's self-satisfaction was based on an overestimation and an excess of investment in the penis, as a source of pride and narcissistic exhibitionism[8]. Phallic narcissism uses a fantasized power of the penis to defend against the memories of early maternal dependence and tender affection against which phallic pride struts. In the years that followed, Freud's phallic narcissism was keenly contested for its excessive grounding in the notion of masculinity.

Perhaps one of the earliest critics of this heavy reliance on masculinity vis-à-vis the phallus was the Calcutta-based self-taught Indian psychoanalyst Girindrasekhar Bose. Bose's twenty-year dialogue with Freud voiced not only his disagreement with the phallic monism of penis envy, but Bose's belief that far from penis envy, it was women's bodies that were envied by men. In his letter to Freud in 1929, Bose wrote, 'The real struggle lies between the desire to be a male and its opposite, the desire to be a female.'[9] Today Freud's phallic narcissism is thought to have reflected the European cultural position of his moment in history, which was that it was preferable to be a man, while Bose's position reflects the ancient Indian cultural position which is that it is preferable to be a woman. Contemporary psychoanalysis would eventually settle on a grass a greener position: while no gender is superior, each gender envies and desires the physical and perceived psychological qualities of the other.

Following Freud, the second major contribution to the understanding of the phallus in psychoanalysis is that of Jacques Lacan, (1966). Lacan's version sees the phallus as a symbol of illusory wholeness, an unattainable state free of desire.[10] For Lacan, children initially feel whole until they become aware of gender difference. This is the moment when a profound sense of lack begins: the child realizes that no one, including herself, is complete. From the desire for completion, comes the wish to be the symbolic phallus symbol that can provide completion to others, particularly the mother in the imagination.[11] For Lacan, everyone fantasizes being a phallus: substituting the neediness of being an incomplete human with a fantasized wholeness symbolized by the phallus.

To differentiate between the positions on the phallus from Freud and Lacan, analysts often use a linguistic distinction: the adjective 'phallic' describes Freud's position (Freud himself used the word phallus rarely but he did make extensive use of the adjective phallic[12]) and connotes an excessive focus on the penis and on masculinity. The noun 'phallus' used by Lacan aims to describe the wish for an uncastrated wholeness, which for Lacan is common to all genders. The Lacanian phallus contains the fantasy that the human could get beyond the loss and desire experienced at the closure of childhood symbiosis during which the child loses the feeling of being 'at one' and begins to experience separateness and difference. The Lacanian phallus, an abstraction, comes into being from some dense theorizing in French psychoanalysis, which attempts to delink the symbolism of the phallus' fullness from the corporeal reality of the male penis.

In dialogue with the Lacanian position where the phallus has a larger aniconic (abstract) meaning unrelated to the male body is another psychoanalytic phallus that comes from the Indian geography. There, the psychoanalyst Sudhir Kakar argues that a shivalingam that arises out of a yoni, not simply an erect penis, is the best visual representation of the idea of completion represented by the phallus. Kakar writes, compellingly:

'The lingam, the aniconic (abstract) representation of the Hindu deity Shiva, is a more appropriate and far-reaching symbol than the phallus for the representation of the psychic constellation discussed [by Lacan]. In its worship in countless homes, roadsides, temples, the phallus in the Shivalingam is always represented as arising out of the yoni, the symbol of female creative energy. The lingam then symbolizes the unity of the male and female and the cosmic energy generated by this union. Iconically, the union is often portrayed in temple sculptures in a starkly sexual language, Shakti straddling the thighs of Shiva in a tight embrace that lasts forever and ever. In its ritual worship in temples and homes, cups of cold milk are poured on the lingam to cool the heat of the energy rising from the union'[13].

Shivalingams are common throughout India.

For Kakar, the phallus represented as the lingam, is a state of narcissistic bisexuality.[14] it is similar to Lacan's phallus, an aniconic (non-bodily and abstract) fantasy that compensates for the vulnerability of gender difference but it is different in that it offers bisexuality rather than uncastrated wholeness as the cure for lack.

Kakar's conception of the phallus–lingam suggests that a normal cultural expression for the cure for the painfulness of sexual difference is to seek refuge in the narcissistic self-sufficiency of bisexuality. As evidence he cites not only the linga–yoni, but also Shiva's form as Hara-Gauri or adhanarishwara, the deity who is half–man and half–woman, one of the most popular subjects in Hindu art and also an expression of a culture that valourizes bisexuality.[15] For Kakar, the aspirational phallus is a respite, however abstract, from a permanent erection: it is best illustrated in the Hindu embelishment of the linga—the Gauripatta or yoni—a vulva-like base from which the phallus just out. Kakar writes, 'For in spite of fantasies of phallic grandeur, the penis itself is of course situated outside the body exposed and vulnerable to injury from without, just as the outgoing self is ever susceptible to the world's encroachments. In situations of aggravated anxiety, the fantasy of the grand invulnerable phallus may not be a sufficient dam against the threat to self-esteem. The solution to the threat is a symbolic withdrawal of the over-cathected penis into oneself, into an internal organ, the vagina where the phallus (and the ego) is safe and beyond harm.'[16] The fact that the symbolic phallus–lingam can be beyond harm, protected by the yoni, as Kakar suggests, promises freedom from death, the ultimate fullness: immortality.

Continents away, ancient Romans worshipped the phallus as a deity and called him Fascinum (from the latin verb 'fascio', which means to bind), from which the modern English 'fascinate' derives.[17] The phallus-shaped fascinum used by the Romans to ward off the evil eye was thought to have a hypnotic power owing to its capacity to draw attention to itself.

The Italian psychoanalyst Carlo Bonomi, (2010), explains that the capacity of the phallus to fascinate, to bind or to command attention, gave it a status in the psyche of ancient Romans. By commanding the positive attention of the eye, they believed that the phallus could resist the evil eye.[18] For psychoanalysis the notion of the evil eye is the destructive part of the self, projected outwards; the phallus therefore represents aliveness, the part of the self that coaxes and convinces against destructiveness

Using examples drawn from his twenty-first century psychoanalytic clinic in Rome, Bonomi suggests that the exhibitionistic use of 'the phallus' can take place by either gender and 'the phallus' can refer to any sheltering function of the body from a perceived malignant disembodied gaze.

Anything that you believe magically hypnotizes and transforms someone else's gaze upon you into a positive one, in other words, for Bonomi, can be a phallus. One of Bonomi's many examples is a young woman whose naked body is her phallus—it fascinates others and makes her feel assured of their continued positive gaze. This woman could not stand to be looked at unless she could reveal her naked body which she believed had the power to charm others and thereby restore her sense of health. Like the fascinum of the ancient Romans, she believed her naked body converted negative impressions into positive ones once she removed her clothes. The woman's behaviour, he points out, was not driven by a sexual desire but by the wish to see the magic effects of her naked body on an enchanted partner[19].

What these definitions have in common is that they believe the phallus' appeal lies in its symbolizing the human wish for a state of fantasy wholeness. For since psychoanalysts, humans' first awareness of 'not-wholeness', lies in the childhood awareness of gender difference. Freud phallicism, Lacan's phallus, Kakar's phallus–lingam and Bonomi's fascinum, are all fantasy cures for the lack created by the awareness of gender difference. Freudian phallic compensation uses the fact that the boy's sexual organ is more overt to proclaim to both genders that it is *the* symbol of sexuality. In assigning more meaning to the penis than it is actually worth, phallic compensation seeks to calm the lack of sexual difference. Lacan's phallus is the symbolic fantasy of uncastrated wholeness that denies the awareness of gender difference. Kakar's phallus–lingam provides a third and distinct kind of fantasy cure: the idea that a primary wholeness represented by the fusion of the yoni and lingam, can be temporarily recovered by a psycho-emotional investment in the bisexual completeness of the phallus–lingam.[20] Bonomi's talisman–phallus cures the problem of separation with the Roman fascinum—it positively draws the attention of the other person into the self so that two feels like one.

If the phallus is a symbol that applies to both genders, why does it use the sexual organ of only one gender?

To accept the importance of the phallus in psychoanalysis ultimately requires thinking symbolically, which requires avoiding the designation of anatomical attributes—penis, clitoris, vagina—and thinking only in terms of the fantasy represented by the phallus-as-symbol.[21] As Lacan, famously said, either you have a penis, or you do not, but in any case you cannot be the phallus.[22] Like other symbols, the choice of phallus as symbol was likely arrived upon via best-available approximation. The iconography of the phallus is not given its power through its anatomical particularities but due to the phallus being a symbol that gains its power from the human investment in what is imagined to be.

The phallus-as-symbol, aims to represent and remember a lost state of human wholeness that is pre-gender. When it comes to gender, men and women alike struggle with the question of loss in ways that are the same as well as different. For both sexes, the ego strength required to bear the arbitrariness of anatomical difference and the underlying essential bisexuality is extraordinary. Both genders, must come to terms with the idea from Freud that 'what constitutes masculinity and femininity is an unknown characteristic which anatomy cannot lay hold of'.[23] If nothing else, the phallus reminds us how unbearable we find the incompleteness catalyzed by gender difference, and reinforces a human aliveness, the notion that the sexual drive, just is, it has no natural object or fixed aim on the other.[24]

The phallus stands up—literally—in objection to the truth that human Eros is marked by a negativity, lack and absence. Cross-culturally, the phallus is represented as uncastrated wholeness, even immortality. Consider this story about the phallus-lingam narrated by Kakar: 'A boy, a great worshipper of Shiva, flung his arms around a lingam and clung tightly to it when Yama, the God of death, came to take him. When Yama tried to pull the boy off, the lingam broke. Defeated, the God of death had to go back empty handed. Shiva was so angry at the damage to the lingam that he cursed Yama that he would no longer be able to carry out his assigned task. Since no one died anymore, the world became overpopulated and Shiva soon had to take his curse back. Here, the lingam represents victory over death'[25].

Despite its anatomical limitation, replete with human hopes of negating death, lack and difference, the phallus as symbol poses the same point to both men and to women: our early experience of wholeness has been lost and we must live with our insatiable desire that is its consequence.

Phallic versus the phallus

While the phallus is associated with the illusory wholeness, a fantasy of return to a state pre-sexual difference, Phallic fantasy uses another method to calm the lack of sexual difference: it makes an excessive investment in the concrete penis to assign more meaning to the penis than it is actually worth. Phallic compensation is characterized by the chauvinistic fantasy of winning, to quote the psychoanalyst Jessica Benjamin, 'what I have is not everything, but it is the only thing (worth having).'[26]

For psychoanalysis, masculine identity is precarious. Analysts agree that the experience of early dependence on a female anatomy—that of the mother—nudges all genders towards the mother as the primary love and erotic object.[27] Heterosexuality for the girl came with a great psychic effort, as does sexual dimorphism—non-genital sexual differences—for the male.[28] The memory of the pleasures and dependency of early infancy is most successfully borne by the ego if the infant grows to be an adult who has the capacity to identify with the mother. By virtue of his dismaying anatomical difference from his mother, the boy child has a disadvantage in his identification with her, a lack that pulls and has to be worked through. How this lack is worked through—whether via love and longing or via rivalry and repudiation of that which has been lost[29]—decides where the boy will find himself on the spectrum of phallic monism–narcissism or phallus longing. The conflict is strengthened when there is a satisfying infant–mother symbiotic period.

According to psychoanalysis, masculinity is not a fact of anatomical difference but something that needs to be created as a response to the wish for symbiosis with the mother—which is a source of anxiety to the ego that struggles to master the loss of that early symbiotic state. As Robert Stoller (1982) explains, the more prolonged and gratifying a mother–son symbiosis, the more a boy's chances of becoming 'masculine' is threatened. To create masculinity, there must be a psychic barrier against the urge to be merged with his mother.[30] The appropriation of the symbol of the phallus serves to insist that the boy is not only different from his mother in bearing, demeanor, psychological traits, and appearance, he is also better than her: as clearly and unequivocally as an erect penis. Thus, as a symbol of masculine fullness, the phallic symbol proclaims itself needed by but not needing femininity in general, and distinct from the early symbiotic relationship of a boy with his mother in particular.

Worldwide, anthropological evidence for the precariousness of masculine identity can be found in contemporary and tribal cultures where masculine identity is bolstered by an excessive investment in the penis, such that it takes on the symbolic order of the phallus. Phallic monism, the adoption of the idea that there was only one organ of value, was a phenomenon that extended far further than Freud. Studying the development of masculine identity cross-culturally, a psychoanalyst, Robert Stoller, and an anthropologist, Gilbert H. Herdt, showcase the Sambia tribe of Papua New Guinea in which a dramatically intensified version of phallic monism forms a lived idiomatic reality in which the entire cultural apparatus is designed to serve the purpose of giving the penis the excess of meaning and importance that turns it into a phallic symbol.

Strength is drunk from father's semen, not mother's milk: the construction of phallic-narcissistic masculinity amidst the Sambia

Phallic masculinity amidst the Sambia, a warlike tribal people of the remote and mountainous Eastern highlands of Papua New Guniea, is oral in many senses of the word. An isolated tribal people numbering some 2,000 warriors—hunters and horticulturists—the Sambia have for generations hunted and harvested in a social structure that functions primarily to perpetuate the warriorhood of its men.[31] In his extensive studies of the Sambia tribe, Gilbert Herdt observed the extraordinary efforts taken by the tribe to fuse masculinity with the phallic. Through every aspect of Sambia life run two concepts steeped with phallic meaning; each designed to deny the men's dependence on women and to insist that there is only one organ of importance and that is the male one.

First is the concept of jerungdu, or strength, that is derived from semen and ingesting semen. In Sambia culture, where there is a long breastfeeding relationship between the mother and child, breast milk is associated with growth but not strength—the reservoirs of a strong warrior comes from semen.[32] The Sambia believe that biologic growth results from ingesting semen and semen equivalent. Babies are considered to grow based on semen accumulations in the mother's womb, breast-feeding is thought to be made possible by a man's inseminations (especially oral) of his wife. After weaning, the child's growth is encouraged by giving nuts from the pandanus tree that are considered a semen equivalent (the tree is tended to by men and the male sweat equity that goes to tending the tree is considered directly related to the tree's productivity). Pre-pubescent boys are initiated into 'monjapi'u'—nourishment through semen—which is considered to bring about the secondary sexual characteristics and build *jerungdu*, and thereby strong warriors. Men replenish their semen by drinking milk-sap from the roots of the padanus tree (the tree is coded female).

A second phallic aspect of Sambia culture is the image of the idealized phallic war leader—the splendid warrior or 'Amoluku'; the Amoluku is like an erect penis, always ready for action. The Amoluku's devalued feminized counterpart is the 'Wussatu' or the 'rubbish man', also known as the 'sweet potato man'. As much as the Amoluku is always hard and ready for action, the 'Wussatu' is soft, worthless. The Wussatu's association to sweet potatoes conjures up a double sign of weakness and feminization: sweet potatoes are 'soft' food and they are cultivated exclusively by women.

Images of valourized hardness and devalued softness dominate every aspect of the Sambia's living. Food, language and community life come together such that the centrality of war victory is constantly being produced and consumed. Thinking, perception and speech are guided by this idiomatic reality in which biological maleness is associated with strength, and phallic hardness, and biological femaleness with the anti-thesis of strength.[33] Three mechanisms do most of the work of overvaluing masculinity: institutionalized fellatio; female avoidance taboos, especially regarding menstrual pollution and fears of semen depletion. Heterosexuality does of course exist, and men are encouraged to take wives in the service of reproduction but a hostility between the genders is cultivated. In the phallic–warrior world of the Sambia, the relentless promotion of hardness has no place for affection between the genders (which would be regarded as soft and feminizing behaviour that compromises the warrior-like qualities of the idealized phallic man).

From a psychoanalytic perspective, the relentless remembering of masculinity always covers up a taboo: the affectionate relationship that was once had with a woman, the mother. The Sambia create and are part of a fantasy system that links speech, physical reality and gender difference with the myth of phallic superiority, but, as Herdt writes, the 'a myth is importance not only for the experiences it embraces but for those it denies'. Underneath the emphasis on phallic strength lies the memory of maternal bonding that must be obliterated by the phallic self-sufficiency of men. The looming memory of the affectionate bond that was held with a woman (the Sambia have an extremely long period of breastfeeding) is reflected in adult Sambia life with concerns about female pollution and terrors of female sexuality that must be overshadowed by an emphasis on the phallic.

Steeped in phallic superiority and concerns of female pollution, the very spatial geography of life in the Sambia hamlet is designed around a separation from and the denial of affectionate ties with women and a substitution of that with male-to-male relationships. Codes on softness and hardness and the insistent remembering of the superiority of hardness and masculinity locate the male clubhouse at an elevation and women are disallowed from walking there—their presence is considered polluting.

The Sambia build a gender identity based on the idealized symbol of an erect penis that is angry and ready for war through ritual. Boys' initiations begin with physical violence that creates anger among the initiates that is considered a salutary bellicosity. In addition, the hard phallus must not yield to a soft female: in keeping with that phallic construction of masculine identity, the Sambia hold the conviction that women deplete men of their strength and eventually even of life itself by robbing—emptying—them, through sexual intercourse, of their male substance, semen.[34] The emphasis on phallic hardness is sustained by keeping the genders separate from a young age, and by creating male initiation rites that first break the boys' connection with their mothers and with all women, and eventually establish connection of boys to men instead. In the early stages of initiation, the boys undergo rituals that make them 'strong and angry' designed to increase their capacity to be warriors. Amongst these anger-making rituals are ritualized nose bleeding, considered salutary as a way of eliminating female contaminants. During the later stages of initiation, the men communicate to the boys the urgent need to consume male semen as an antidote to the 'soft food' (including breast milk) that was fed to them by their mothers. By supplementing the 'soft' (breast milk) with the 'hard' (semen), manhood is conferred upon the young boys. Men are encouraged to release anger by relaxing their tight penises as dominant fellates for the younger initiates. Boys are paired up with older men in a ritualized fashion, after which, in the mechanics of fellatio are demonstrated with a bamboo flute to younger boys in a secret ceremony.

Secrecy makes the affective power of the phallic fantasy available while hiding its fantasy basis. The fantasy in this case is that of male parthenogenesis[35]: the fantasy that males can reproduce by themselves and that women can therefore be altogether dispensed with. The purpose of valourizing male-to-male fellatio in concert with male semen as a superior substitute for mother's milk, is an act of imaginary recreation that transports the boy from a world in which he is linked to his mother and women, to one in which he is independent from women in all matters. The Sambia men do return to heterosexuality with their betrothed female partners whom they marry, but the emphasis in these marriages is on reproduction and on masculine virility demonstrated through reproduction. The hostility between the genders and the inferiority of women continues to pervade after marriage, nowhere more clear in Herdt's interviews where Sambia men frequently express an ignorance or disinterest in the female orgasm. Through a combination of biological difference emphasized to declare male superiority, strict gender roles, institutionalized homosexuality, and above all an oral (in both senses of the word) idiomatic reality that valourizes semen over breastmilk, phallic narcissism is established as male identity and the connection to the mother and things female-repudiated.

With my love, I give you masculinity: phallic longing amongst the Dorian Greeks

For the Greek-speaking Dorians, who invaded the Greek mainland around 1200 BC, the anxiety about the precariousness of masculinity was allayed via ritualized, love relationships between pre-pubescent young boys and older men, considered the route to pleasurable masculinity. These love relationships were not private erotic enterprises; they were public, state-sanctioned and regarded to be of ethical and social importance.[36] Pre-pubescent boys, learned to be men, by a process of identification with an older man; facilitated by an affectionate and socially celebrated sexual relationship. An example of such a relationship is seen in Danish psychoanalyst Thorkil Vanggaard's (1969) description of an engraving on a black-figure Attican vase from the sixth century BCE.[37]

On the vase appear a man and a boy in conversation. The man, of large and visibly powerful musculature, and phallus erect, addresses himself to the small slender visibly younger boy. The boy is beardless and his penis soft. With one hand, the older man extends a wreath, the sign of love in Greek iconography, towards the youth. In the other hand, the man holds a powerful dog on a leash—the dog is a sign of a phallus in the Greek iconography. Thorkil, drawing from the philologist Eric Bethe (1863–1940) explains that the message is of the older man as the giver of phallic attribute to the younger. The dog that the older man holds back is the aggressive element of the phallus over which the older man is master, a form of mastery that will, it is implied, be the inheritance of the younger man as he receives love and tutelage from the elder.[38] This is the promise of the Erastes (lover)–Eromenos (beloved boy) relationship, available in the normal—that is to say, accepted and expectable—homosexuality amongst the Dorian Greeks. The initiation of pre-pubescent boys into this aspect of

masculinity carries with it the promise that the warrior-like attributes of the phallus along with the other mysteries of masculinity will be transmitted to them during the course of the relationship[39].

The attributes of masculinity, included 'Arēte'—a word that conveys a concept of nobility and honour that held a critical place in the Greek spiritual culture.[40] Thought to be the driving force behind human character, Aretē was a combination of physical prowess, mental qualities like courage, fidelity to duty, obedience and solidarity with fellows, honour, fairness, reliability as a host and as a guest; these qualities led ultimately to a man's fame and distinction and were related to nobility testified to by ancestry. Aretē depended upon who one's fathers and forefathers had been. Yet, while Aretē is a form of inheritance combined with upbringing, it can also be acquired in the Erastēs–Erómenos love between boys and men that the Dorians believed created skillful and competent male leaders through the transmission of Aretē. Aretē transmitted as the essence of masculinity, is the subtle correlate of the Sambia idea of jerungdu, or strength, that is derived from semen and ingesting semen. For the Dorian state to sanction the paiderastic relationship, the criteria were a considerable age difference which gave an ethical basis for the relationship rooted in manliness and honour—as Bethe, puts it 'The qualities of the man, his aretē, are in some way transmitted to the beloved boy through love'[41] or as Aristophanes says in Plato's *Symposium*, 'Only those play their role in the state who in their boyhood experienced a man's love.'[42]

If we return here to the psychoanalytic definition of the phallus as a fantasy phenomenon that arises as a response to the painful lack experienced from the awareness of sexual difference, Dorian love suggests that the phallus is available, for a period of time, during which the painfulness of sexual difference can be consoled by the pleasures of sexual sameness alongside an ongoing heterosexuality. Sambia phallicism resembles Freudian phallic–narcissism: it aggrandizes the penis to a phallus and repudiates the vagina insisting on only one organ of importance. Dorian love palliates the lack of sexual difference with the fullness of state-sanctioned male bisexuality. And, if the Sambia (and

Freudian) phallic narcissism is keen to erase the memory of the mother, then the Dorian phallus longing seeks to revive the memory of the early dyadic father, to balm the pain of paternal absence.

If the phallus and all of what is phallic is always a marker of lack, a missing pre-gender human wholeness, then the subtle difference between the Sambia and Dorian positions offers a further insight into group behaviour and the phallus. While Dorian masculinity has in common with Sambia masculinity an exposure to physical hardship, a focus on aggression and the transmission of phallic masculinity between men, what is different between the two is that while the Sambia seek to repudiate the mother–son bond in a substitution of semen for mother's milk and an emphasis on the polluting aspects of femininity, the Dorians draw upon the imagery and valourize the father–son relationship, to confer masculinity as longing for men rather than as a repudiation of women. The Sambia culture of oral masculine transmission in combination with misogynistic views of feminine pollution aim to crystalize masculinity by emphasizing phallicity and forgetting the mother, while Dorian Erastes–Eramenos relationships with their focus on transmission across the generations, aim to crystalize masculinity by memorializing the father. The Dorian examples seems to argue that it was not that the early symbiotic relationship with the mother was overwhelming for masculine identity but that the absence of an early symbiotic relationship with the father is what was lacking. Thus while Sambia relationships refuse an identification—that with the women and the mother—Dorian relationships reinstate a refused identification, the erotic relationship of the boy with his father that is denied as much by culture as was denied by early psychoanalysis.

Certain elements of Dorian love are present to this day in modern India too, in the Guru–Disciple (Guru–Shishya) relationship. Within the dynamic of student and Master–Teacher is present the yearning for parents of both genders, a desire for merger such that the Guru's knowledge and self can suffuse that of the disciple, and a phallus longing for wholeness beyond difference. When Kakar describes the closeness of the Guru-Disciple relationship his words are tinged with the undertones of the Lacanian phallus: 'The sought-for intimacy is of an archaic nature, before the birth of language which separates and bifurcates'[43] and the Guru–Disciple relationships touches 'the depressive core at the base of human life from which a self first emerged and which lies beyond words and interpretations.'[44] While the manifest discourse in the Guru–Disciple relationship is about the merger of soul, Kakar suggests, that the latent fantasies of the disciple most likely also incude the merger of bodies—the disciple's imagined secret wish is to ingest the purest and innermost substance ingestible from the teacher: his semen.[45]

Coda: The future of phallic and phallus

Based in the emotional experience of the clinic and the products of popular culture some Euro-American psychoanalysts (such as Benton, 1995) have argued that that the phallus as a symbol is losing and will further lose its meaning as the twenty-first century progress.[46] The suggestion here is that human beings are more comfortable with the chaos of difference, more able to bear separation, and less interested in having phallic authorities that steer them through this chaos.[47] It's a position that is squarely located in a geographical region—North America—that embraces secular modernity. In contrast, I would like to use this last section to argue that phallus longing will continue to have meaning in geographical regions where cultural and religious experiences that celebrate states of fullness (the phallus) and aesthcticize states of yearning (phallus–longing).

Culture and cultural positions on wholeness, sexual fluidity and grief, set the stage for how individuals organize themselves around the phallus and the phallic. It is the collective imagination of the group that infuses the phallus with meaning: The intervention of the group makes the loss of wholeness a common human heritage. The group provides a shared understanding that the individual ego alone does not have the strength required to bear the arbitariness of sexual difference and the loss of wholeness. The phallus and the phallic represent efforts made by the cultural apparatus to symbolize, and thereby cope with the ineffable panoply of painful conflicts related to separation: the wish to reclaim the wholeness of early life; the pain of separation in the awareness of difference; the anxiety that desire's aim is unknown and the confusion of misleading visible anatomical difference.

The modern condition has tended to push towards the valourization of phallic narcissism—that is self-satisfaction and a denial of loss and difference—for both genders. Here the phallic, symbolized by the demands of a relentless erection—entitlement to desire satisfaction, intolerance of loss and denial of inequality—is positioned as strength and power. One has to look no further than a cultural product like Facebook, where positivity, self-sufficiency and plenitude are valourized, while lack and the feelings associated including need, envy, fear, guilt and helplessness are more likely to be denied. While the phallic in modernity is often left unsymbolized, the power conferred by phallic possession, the demonstration of plenty, and the denial of lack, is ubiquitous; the fact that this phallic ubiquitousness is underwritten in the imagination by the symbol of a penis in relentless erection, in Stoller's words: 'goes some way towards explaining social phenomena which have given men greater power and status.'[48]

The counter to such a culture of phallic denial of what has been lost would be a culture of acknowledged longing for the phallus, what collectively psychoanalysts might call the longing for uncastrated wholeness (Lacan) or narcissistic bisexuality (Kakar). This longing is more commonly acknowledged as the human craving for fascinating states of attention that bind the anxiety of separation. Here it would be remiss not to mention religious and mystical enchantment and aesthetic arrest as areas of human existence that recreate the memory of what the analysts call the phallus—a unitary state of pre-wholeness—in psychic experience.

As a fact of both its history and geography, Euro-American psychoanalysis has been reluctant to narrate the benefits of religious states as a return to wholeness. Psychoanalysis was born in Europe as the new secular religion of modernity, which allowed more freedom to comment on the phallic (forms of monism, intolerance and insistence on only one truth) rather than phallus longing for a return to unitary states, present in all religions. Arguing in favour of the human attraction for the psychic states offered by religion, Kakar locates religious longing alongside those natural phenomena, art forms or extraordinary moments that, 'lights up the narrow, mundane world of daily existence, a world which has always been inadequate to our experience and unequal to bear the burden of our hopes.'[49] Argued thus, mystical states in religion are on a continuum with the illusory wholeness that has preoccupied poets and philosophers from across the world. To the poet, wholeness is illusory not because it is not real, but because it is temporary. Receiving wholeness while temporarily shutting off the awareness of its temporariness is a pre-requisite for the experience of delight: As the fifth-century Indian poet Bhatrihari writes, 'Everything is delightful if you agree to think not even a little of how transient it all is'.[50]

The mystical aspects of almost every religion, offer access to the wholeness and unitary consciousness promised by the symbol of the phallus. Variously called *samadhi* (Hindus), *satori* (Zen) and *fana* (Sufi)[51] amongst just a few names, the appeal of mystical states in which all differentiations vanish, and subject and object become one, is a cross-cultural phenomenon but in modern times has stronger roots in the geography of Asia. The popularity of the mystico-religious experience of wholeness unfolds in the collective imagination in two ways: first, the pleasures of the state of wholeness is sung as the greatest pleasure, a source of heightened intrapsychic and bodily sensation that absorbs all other experience; second the painful yearning implicit in the experience of difference is valourized mythopoetically as a salutary experience of aestheticized loss.

Consider first the valourization of wholeness in the Indian geography. In his introduction to his translation of the Upanishads, Eknath Easwaran introduces what he calls the science of meditation by quoting Aldous Huxley, 'all science is a reduction of multiplicities to unities'[52] adding that the vedic hymns he is about to translate 'are steeped in the conviction of rita, a order that pervades creation, a oneness to which all diversities can be referred.'[53] For Easwaran, wholeness is not only desirable, it is also scientifically attainable, indeed it is the purpose of science. Likewise, in attestation to wholeness as the natural order of things, the four-line Sanskrit verse that prefaces the over 1500-year-old Isha Upanishad is still frequently chanted by Indian schoolchildren: 'All this is full. All that is full. From fullness, fullness comes. When fullness is taken from fullness, fullness still remains.'[53] Intense states of longing for union and fullness and their expression, find an exalted place in both religious and secular culture via the arts, particularly music. Asserting and restating the natural order of fullness rather than difference in the oral culture, unites the major Indian religions, and continues the contribution to the Indian idiomatic reality in which a return to wholeness still occupies an affectively hopeful space in the collective imagination.

Whether or not the phallus will continue to have a meaning in a particular geographic region depends, I would argue on the counter solution proposed by that regional group to the agony of individual separateness. To reiterate, phallus longing, is a group form that mobilizes the collective imagination in a way that is protective to the human enterprise. If the wish to return to a state of oneness before difference is dismissed as a possibility, then it repudiates the human wish for a unitary state, requiring surrender to the chaos of difference without hope of return to wholeness. To say the phallus is no longer relevant repudiates the wish for wholeness. Like other repudiations, the repudiation of the wish for wholeness risks leaking out as phallic aggression: chaos of the state of separateness and difference risks manifesting in painful and unbearable psychic states. Religious enchantment and cultural products that facilitate the experience of yearning for a lost wholeness may owe their appeal to the consolation they offer for the loss of what psychoanalysts call the symbol of the phallus.

THE PHALLUS IN EUROPE

Johan Mattelaer

The study of phallicism is the study of religion. No one who neglects the study of phallic worship can hope to secure any adequate understanding of the origin of religion.

—George Ryley Scott, *Phallic Worship*

Since prehistoric times, the phallus has been present anywhere and everywhere in Europe: in Greek, Roman and Celtic temples and streets, and in every house. The phallus was simply there and nobody worried about or was indignant about it's presence—it was so obvious to have it around in daily life that nobody paid attention to it or wrote about it!

In the introduction of *The Reign of the Phallus*, Eva C. Keuls states: 'The story of phallic rule at the root of Western civilization has been suppressed as a result of the near-monopoly that men have held in the field of Classics, by neglect of rich pictorial evidence, by prudery and censorship, and by a misguided desire to protect an idealized image of Athens (and Rome).'

Till very recently, almost without exception, the modern critic viewed phallicism strictly in relation to the twentieth-century moralistic and ethical ideals. This essential and basic difference between ancient and modern ideas of morality and ethics has constituted one of the major difficulties in dealing with phallicism.

The fact that phallic worship has, for so many generations, been looked at as something to be hidden and the fact that it received ecclesiastical condemnation where there was no downright denial of its existence and in the taboo so continuously and ecumenically imposed upon its expression and, last but not least, in the feeling that any discussion concerning it was tantamount to an admission of bawdy tastes, no doubt lie the main reasons for the neglect which the subject has received by writers and historians generally (G.R. Scott).

Naked woman handling two olisboi or dildos detail on a Greek kylix.

Even the eleventh edition of the Encyclopedia Britannica contains only a short article of fifty-one lines on phallicism. In the fourteenth edition even less space has been devoted to the subject: a sum total of seventeen lines!

The first mention of phallicism in post-Renaissance western Europe was in a letter written by Sir William Hamilton, His Majesty's Minister at the Court of Naples, to Sir Joseph Banks, baron, president of the Royal Society and the other person residing at Isernia in December 1781.

At the time that this letter was written, erotic objects and paintings were discovered during the archeological excavations in Pompeii and Herculaneum. Those discoveries shocked the Western world! And soon, because of morality and prudery the phallus was condemned and seen as very negative.

The Letter from Isernia by Sir William Hamilton (December 1781):

> Sir,
>
> .... I had long ago discovered, that the Women and Children of the lower class, at NAPLES, and in its neighborhood, frequently wore, as an ornament of dress, sort of Amulets, (which they imagine to be a preservative from the mal occhii, evil eyes or enchantment) exactly similar to those which were worn by the ancient Inhabitants of this Country for the very same purpose, as likewise for their supposed invigorating influence; and all of which have a relation to the Cult of PRIAPUS. Struck with this conformity in modern and ancient superstition, I made a collection of both the ancient, and modern Amulets of this sort, and placed them together in the BRITISH MUSEUM, where they remain.
>
> The modern Amulet most in vogue, represents a hand clinched, with the point of the thumb thrust betwixt the index and middle

finger; the next is a shell; and the third is a half-moon. These Amulets (except the shell, which is usually worn in its natural state) are most commonly made of silver, but sometimes of ivory, coral, amber, crystal, or some curious gem, or pebble. We have a proof of the hand above described having a connexion with PRIAPUS, in a elegant small idol of bronze of that Divinity, now in the ROYAL MUSEUM of PORTICI, and which was found in the ruins of HERCULANEUM: it has an enormous Phallus, and, with an arch look and gesture, stretches out its right hand in the form above mentioned; and which probably was an emblem of consummation: and as a further proof of it, the Amulet which occurs most frequently amongst those of the Ancients (next to that which represents the simple Priapus, is such a hand united with the Phallus; of which you may see several specimens in my collection in the BRITISH MUSEUM. One in particular, I recollect, has also the half-moon joined to the hand and Phallus; which half-moon is supposed to have an allusion to the female menses. The shell, or concha veneris, is evidently an emblem of the female part of generation.

It is very natural then to suppose, that the Amulets representing the Phallus alone, so visibly indecent, may have been long out of use in this civilized capital; but I have been assured, that it is but very lately that the Priests have put an end to the wearing of such Amulets in CALABRIA, and other distant Provinces of this Kingdom.

A new road having been made last year from this Capital to the Province of ABRUZZO, passing through the City of ISERNIA (anciently belonging to the SAMNITES, and very populous), a person of a liberal education, employed in that work, chanced to be at ISERNIA just at the time of the celebration of the Feast of the modern PRIAPUS, St. Como; and having been struck with the singularity of the ceremony, so very similar to that which attended the ancient Cult of the GOD of the GARDENS, and knowing my taste for antiquities, told me of it. From this Gentleman's report, and from what I learnt on the spot from the Governor of ISERNIA himself, having gone to that City on purpose in the month of February last, I have drawn up the following account, which I have reason to believe is strictly true. I did intend to have been present at the Feast of St. COSMO this year; but the indecency of this ceremony having probably transpired, from the country's having been more frequented since the new road was made, orders have been given, that the Great Toe of the Saint should no longer be exposed. The following is the account of the Fête of St. COSMO and DAMIANO, as it actually was celebrated at ISERNIA, on the confines of ABRUZZO, in the Kingdom of NAPLES, so late as in the year of our Lord 1780...

... This Church is dedicated to ST COSMOS and DAMIANUS. One of the days of the Fair, the relicks of the Saints are exposed, and afterwards carried in procession from the Cathedral of the City to this Church, attended by a prodigious concourse of people. In the city, and at the fair, Ex-voti of wax, representing the male parts of generation, of various dimensions, some even of the length of a palm, are publickly offered to sale. There are also waxen vows, that represent other parts of the body mixed with them; but of those there are few in comparison of the number of the Priapi. The devout distributers of these vows carry a basket full of them in one hand, and hold a plate in the other to receive the money, crying aloud, "St. COSMO"and DAMIANO!" If you ask the price of one, the answer is, più ci metti, più meriti: "The more you give, the more's the merit." ...

The cross, made from gold, probably worn by an early Christian bishop during formal ceremonies, combines phalluses with female genitalia.

A

LETTER

FROM

SIR *WILLIAM HAMILTON*, &c.

Naples, Dec. 30, 1781.

SIR,

HAVING laſt year made a curious diſcovery, that in a Province of this Kingdom, and not fifty miles from its Capital, a ſort of

A 2 devo-

The letter by Sir William Hamilton dated, 30 December 1781, with elaborate phallic images. Printed by T. Spilsburg, Snowhill in 1786.

A wall fresco depicting Hermes, the god of trade and commerce, but also of sex and fertility, with his extremely enlarged penis.

... The Vows are chiefly presented by the female sex; and they are seldom such as represent legs, arms &c. but most commonly the male parts of generation. The Person who was at this Fête in the year 1780, and who gave me this account (the authenticity of every article of which has since been fully confirmed to me by the Governor of ISERNIA), told me also, that he heard a Woman say at the time she presented a vow, like that which is represented in Plate I.Fig.I. Santo Cosimo Benedetto, cosi lo voglio: “Blessed St. COSMO, let it be like this;” another, St.Cosimo, ti ringrazio: “St. COSMO, I thank you.”
...:...

I am, SIR,
with great truth and regard,
Your most obedient humble Servant,
William Hamilton.

Around the same time, a very remarkable cross was found in San-Agatha di Gaeti near Naples. The cross first belonged to the collection Beresford Fletcher and later to Ambroise Ruschenberger from Boston, USA. This golden cross was made of four phalluses, with a circle of female organs around the center and a suspender at the top. Since the cross was in pure gold, it must have been in the possession of an important sacerdotal person, perhaps a bishop.

The discovery of erotic art in Pompeii and Herculaneum left the archaeologists with a dilemma: between the mores of sexuality in Ancient Rome and the Counter-Reformation in Europe. Both Pompeii and Herculaneum were ancient Roman cities in the bay of Naples that were buried under volcanic ash and pumice when Mount Vesuvius erupted in 79 AD. The site was lost until it was discovered in 1599. The architect Domenico Fontana was called in. He unearthed a few more frescoes, then covered them over again; nothing more came of the discovery. Fontana's covering over the paintings has been seen both as a broad-minded act of preservation for later times and as censorship in view of the frequent sexual content of such paintings, as he would have known the hedonistic nature of the paintings and artefacts. While Herculaneum was properly rediscovered only in 1738 by workmen digging for the foundations of a summer palace for the King of Naples, Charles of Bourbon, Pompeii was rediscovered as the result of intentional excavations in 1748 by the Spanish military engineer Rocque Joaquin de Alcubierre. Many frescos, statues and objects that have been discovered in these sites were hidden in secret places. For instance, a wall fresco depicting Hermes, the ancient god of trade and commerce, shown with an extremely enlarged penis was covered with plaster. In 1819, when King Francis visited the Pompeii exhibition at the Naples National Archaeological Museum with his wife and daughter, he was so embarrassed by the erotic artwork that he decided to have it locked away in a so-called secret cabinet 'gabinetto segreto', a gallery within the museum accessible only to 'people of mature age and respected morals'. For the next hundred years, the secret part of the gallery was re-opened, closed, re-opened again and then closed again. The Naples 'Secret Museum' was briefly made accessible again at the end of the 1960s (the time of the sexual revolution) and was finally re-opened for viewing in 2000.

Phallic stones, objects and paintings in prehistoric Europe

Penis is not phallus. The later is a perfectly apt word for the erect organ and all symbolic meanings that attach to that state.

—David M. Friedman, *A Mind of Its Own.*

Menhirs are tall standing stones, often in the form of a phallus. They date back to a time when no written records existed. The name 'menhir' is derived from the Breton words maen, meaning stone, and hir, meaning high. Initially, menhirs probably served a religious function. When a number stand together, they are usually arranged in a circle or square, called cromlechs. They are among the oldest expressions of monumental cults and culture. Menhirs can still be seen at numerous locations in Western Europe, particularly in France and Portugal.

In the prehistoric period, the erotic and social aspects of man were closely interlinked. The prehistoric human being was driven by the need to survive in a hostile environment and survival depended on food and fertility. Paleolithic artists created objects designed to exert a magical influence on human fertility: female and male figures with exaggerated genitalia, and striking phalluses in

Stone forest, Varna Province, Bulgaria (right) and a mehnir at Champ Dolent, Dol de Bretagne, France (left).

Rock paintings from the Bronze Age in Fossum, Bohuslän, Sweden. The nude warriors are depicted with an obvious phallus.

particular. Ithyphallic images and objects were far from scarce in the prehistoric period, and clearly indicate the symbolic value attached to them: strength, power, virility and fertility.

The oldest anatomically-precise image of a phallus dates from the Perigordian period, about 30,000–35,000 years ago. Findings from the Paleolithic era (up to 20,000 BC) show predominantly ritualistic images of men and women with the head of a bird. From the Neolithic period onwards, depictions of the phallus and ithyphallic figures became more frequent.

George Ryley Scott points out that: 'The recognition that man played a part in creation was not necessarily associated with the sex act. My contention is that, without exception, the worship of sex by all primitive races originated in the pleasure associated with coitus, and not in any clearly conceived notion that intercourse would produce children. The sex act gave pleasure to the gods.' But on the other hand, Jacques Dupuis suggests in his book *Au nom du Père* that the veneration of the phallus could perhaps be linked with the discovery of fatherhood, which was not such an obvious concept among primitive cultures. The development of the cultural connotation of the phallus in prehistoric times is part of a very specific male mythology, which was perhaps passed on during initiation rites for boys or in the context of hunting. This mythology would probably also be part of the shaman's repertoire. Gradually, the erect penis came to be a symbol of power.

This rock painting from the post Paleolithic era found in the Magura caves in the Vidin Province, northwestern Bulgaria, shows several ithyphallic dancers.

It is only from the Magdalenian period, around 13,000–6,000 BC onwards, that images of the phallus become frequent. There is ample evidence from the Bronze Age in Scandinavia (1,600–400 BC) indicating the importance of the phallic symbol in the religion of the period. There is one factor common to all the male figures in ritual scenes depicted, all were portrayed with an erect penis.

Images of the phallus are found whenever strength, skill, the sublime and the holy needed to be expressed. And so, many meanings come together in the one graphic image of the phallus. Much of what the phallic symbol represents has nothing to do with the sexual act itself—strength in combat, for example, or skill in hunting or good luck at sea. This is highlighted very clearly in the Stone Age drawings in Bohuslän in southern Sweden and Bardal in Norway. In these drawings ithyphallic men are depicted in the midst of hunting scenes. More examples of this can be seen in the Magura caves in the Vidin Province in northwestern Bulgaria where several ithyphallic dancers from the post-Paleolithic era can be found.

Phallic Worship in Ancient Egypt and the Middle East

The phallus is really the symbol of the Creator in mankind and we find his worship at the origin of all religions.

—Alain Daniélou, *Le Phallus*

The first civilizations which have influenced Western culture were located in Asia Minor, around the Tigris and Euphrates rivers: the Sumerian, Babylonian, Assyrian and Mesopotamian cultures.

Özgen Acar states that the phallus cult originated in Anatolia, currently known as Turkey. At Göbekli Höyük in the Urfa Province of southeastern Anatolia, a 40cm-tall statue of a father god with an exaggerated penis was found. The statue dates back 11,000–12,000 years before our time, when ceramics were not yet in use.

Bull cults and phallic cults

More phallic cultures are also found west of Anatolia, as in Tbilisi in Georgia and in Metsamar in Georgia. Armenia's *Fertile Crescent* was located in the land between rivers, the famous Tigris and Euphrates.

In early Mesopotamia, the most important gods were Enlil and Enki, both descendants of the old upper god Anoe. The virility of Enki was emphasized, he was associated with the 'Bull of Heaven' and established world order. Enlil, chief of the Sumerian pantheon, was believed to have 'stimulated his male organ to that great mountain and emptied (his seed), both winter and summer, into the womb that brings fertility to the country.' In other verses from 3000 BC, we can read that the god Enki, or his phallus was the creative power. The following lines from *Myths of Enki, the Crafty God*, show this:

Ceremonial phallic sculpture from the grave of Phrygian princess Emali dating to eighth century BC.

After Father Enki lifted his eyes over the Euphrates,
he stood up full of lust like an attacking bull,

The ithyphallic Assyrian god Baal Peor, who later became the god Bes in Asia Minor.

lifted his penis, ejaculated,
and filled the Euphrates with flowing water.

Six lines later Enki does the same for the Tigris:

He lifted his penis, he brought the bridal gifts,
like a great wild bull he trilled the heart of the Tigris,
(and stood by) as it gave birth.

In Asia, Europe and Africa, the bull god was the centerpiece of the bull cult and known variously as Marduk (Babylonia), Enki (Mesopotamia), Minotaur (Crete, Greece), Apis (Egypt) and the horned Pashupati—the lord of animals—of the Shaivite civilization of the Indus Valley. The bull god's symbol was the phallus, and in the East, the bull was often depicted as the partner of the great goddess of fertility, thereby representing the virile principle of generation and invincible force. Numerous pictorial and plastic representations of the bull have been uncovered, many of these designed to be worn as a charm or amulet. In Egypt, bull cults were popular from at least the First Dynasty. The powerful and virile bull was associated with the pharaoh, who sometimes took the epithet strong bull of his mother. As early as 3100 BC, the king is depicted in the form of a bull. The most famous of the bull cults is undoubtedly that of the Apis bull or Hapi-ankh. The bull was the incarnation of a god, but unlike the other animal totems, the Apis was thought to host the god himself.

Later, in the Middle East, it was predominantly the god Baal Peor, later known as Bes, who was worshipped in an ithyphallic form, although Ashur, the ithyphallic god of the Assyrians, was represented even earlier in the form of an upright stone.

After these ancient cultures and religions in the Middle East, Western civilization was inspired from another civilization which dwelled at the narrow strip of fertile land along the banks of the river Nile: Ancient Egypt.

Limestone statue of the dancing god, Bes, with a prominent phallus.

For the ancient Egyptians, at the beginning of time, nothing existed but Nun (the original waters). The father god, Atum of Heliopolis, could not even find a place to stand on. But Atum grew and grew until he was as tall as a hill, and on this hill, with his phallus, he engendered first himself (he who existed by himself):

> Atum's penis creates all life, divine and mortal, through this act of sacred masturbation, starting with the god of air and the goddess of moisture, who emerged from his semen.
>
> After Atum engendered himself he gave birth to his two children: Shu (the air) and Tephnet (the water). Then Tephnet bore Geb or Keb (the earth) and Nut (the heavens), and they in turn bore the two divine couples: Osiris and Isis, and Seth and Nephthys.

With the gods Min, Amon-Re and Osiris, the phallus became an institution in Egyptian mythology. The erect penis became a sign of good fortune and masculine strength, which could even overcome death by joining the great phallus of Osiris in heaven. Amon-Re of Karnak, the creator of all life and the king of all gods, with his double crown of feathers and solar disc, was therefore always represented as an ithyphallic figure since the days of the Middle Kingdom. This aspect of Amon-Re was derived from the god of fertility, Min of Koptos (north of Luxor, now called Qift). Min was originally portrayed without a crown of feathers or a solar disc, but from about 3000 BC onwards limestone images of Min were always ithyphallic. Images of Min as a god of fertility show him with two arms. When bestowing his life-giving sperm, he is depicted in profile, as figures were always represented in Egyptian bas-reliefs, in these only one arm can be seen, and the other is assumed to be supporting the phallus. This gesture of the left hand holding the penis is reminiscent of the ancient Egyptian creation myth, in which Atum, the original god, creates the world by swallowing his own sperm and begetting the first life within himself.

(Top, right) Amon-Re of Karnak, the king of the gods, with his crown of feathers. His left hand, not shown here, holds his penis, is reminiscent of the ancient Egyptian creation myths in which Atum, the original god, creates the world by swallowing his own semen. (Top left) an Egyptian papyrus showing the copulation of Geb (the god of Earth) and Nut (the god of Heaven).

Penile sheaths, which can be found in many cultures, can also be found in Egypt. In fact, the oldest penile sheaths can be found on pre- and proto dynastic Egyptian figures from around 3000 BC. A well-known example is the black marble figure which explorer William McGregor (1848–1937) brought from his Egyptian expedition during the late 1800s from Naqada in Upper Egypt. The sheath dates back to about 3100 BC. Another penile sheath from that same period is in ivory.

In many Egyptian temples, ithyphallic figures were set up as votive offerings so that the donor would be blessed with children. In Luxor and Abu Simbel, dozens of ithyphallic images have been carved in bas-relief in the temple walls and in the shrines dedicated to Min.

During that time, the most important religious feast of the season was that of Min, the god of procreation. He is depicted as a veiled human figure with a permanent erection. His crown is a flat, round cap with a ribbon and two tall plumes on top—the same as worn by the god Amon in Luxor, with whom he is closely connected. The climax of the feast of Min was the procession with the image of the god. This devotional image was placed on a platform covered with a red cloth scattered with sequins and borne on the shoulders of twenty priests. The statue of Min, with the phallus painted black for emphasis, represented the land of Egypt and above all the fertility of the land. A white bull, the holy animal of Min, headed the procession in which the royal family, the priests, musicians and military escort took part.

In the Ptolemaic period, the figure of Bes with a huge phallus was venerated and later imported to Rome as Priapus. This was due to intercultural and interreligious contact between countries around the Mediterranean sea. In the Late Egyptian period, the Greek god Dionysus was also celebrated as described by Herodotus in *The Histories*, Book II, 48:

The feast of Dionysus is celebrated by the Egyptians in the same way as by the Hellenes in almost all things except choral dances, but instead of the phallus they have invented another contrivance, namely figures of about a cubit in height worked by strings, which women carry about the villages, with the privy member made to move and not much less in size than the rest of the body: and a flute goes before and they follow singing the praises of Dionysus. As to the reason why the figure has this member larger than is natural and moves it, though it moves no other part of the body, about this there is a sacred story told.

But the phallus was not only a religious phenomenon. The Egyptian Museum of Turin, Italy, has since 1825 an erotically papyrus with sex scenes and a man with a hug phallus in their collection. It is a papyrus roll with a satirical part of 88 cm and an erotically part of 173cm. It is from the Late Period and was found in Deir el Medina but is severely damaged. When Jean-François Champollion, the discoverer of Egyptian hieroglyphs, saw the papyrus in 1824, he protested and exclaimed: *peintures d'une obscénité monstrueuse et que me donnent une bien singulière idée de la gravité et de la sagesse égyptienne* (paintings of a monstrous obscenity that give me a very singularly idea of Egyptian seriousness and wisdom). Morality has changed but sexuality remains the same!

An ivory figure with a penis sheath from Egypt, 3100 BC.

A wall painting in the house of the Vetii in Pompeii, depicting a man—perhaps Priapus himself—weighing his phallus against a bag of gold.

The phallus and Priapus in Ancient Greece and Rome

Phallicism, even in its original crudity, implied something more than the mere worship of the male and female external genitalia, developing into a religious concept which was wider, more profound and more comprehensive than that connected with any specific contemporary faith.

—George Ryley Scott

A marble statue of Herm with an erect phallus.

Ancient Greece

In Ancient Greece herms—a square column with the head of an old man and an erect phallus—were erected near temples and houses. Herms or 'hermae' with inscriptions were also found at crossroads, where they served as signposts. Hermae were believed to provide protection, but the erect penis also symbolized Athenian power— some herms were erected to honor important men. After the Greeks defeated the Persians at Eion in 475 BC, a memorial in the form of three marble hermae was built in the Agora of Athens and the victory was symbolized by three stone erections.

In many ways, the hermae served many cultural functions too. In 415 BC, Athens was shaken by a scandal. Before the Athenian army left for Sicily, a group of conspirators smashed off the erections on hundreds of the city's herms. Whether this was a drunken prank or, as Eva Keuls writes, an antiwar protest by Athenian women, there is no disputing the event's meaning to Athenian men. The city was emasculated—a terrifying omen! That the Sicilian invasion failed and ultimately hastened Athenians defeat by Sparta only confirmed those beliefs.

The Greek link between the phallus and power was noted by Kallixeinos of Rhodos around 275 BC with an eyewitness account of a Dionysian festival in

Greece is full of phallic structures and art, like this Greek woman seen pouring water over terracotta phalluses (left)) and marble phalluses found in the temple of Dionysus on the island of Delos (right).

Alexandria in which a golden phallus, 180-feet long and topped by a gold star, was carried through the city as people listened to poems sung in its honour.

Dionysus was the son of Zeus and his beloved Semele. When Semele was burnt to ashes, Zeus was able to save her unborn child Dionysus. Thereafter, Dionysius became a very popular god and was honoured each year in Athens with seven festivals, each marked by a procession of phalloi (replicas of a phallus) held by phallophoroi (the bearers of a large phallus), who walked through the city, holding aloft their wooden erections, drank wine and sang lewd songs. Countless images of the phallus—which the Romans called 'virilia'—were carried in the procession, and the participants themselves wore huge artificial phalluses. Many Attic wine cups, amphora and vases are painted with erotically and phallic decorations.

Rome

Crede mihi, non est mentula quod digitus.
'Believe me, you cannot command this organ as though it was your finger.'
—Martial, *Epigrams*, VI, 23

The Romans never quite knew how to react to the Greek gods in human form. In the beginning, the Roman worshipping was a mixture of Etruscan and Latin elements, influenced by Hellenic, Syrian, Egyptian and Persian religious ideas.

According to Davenport the Roman worship of Priapus—the god of fertility—comes from the Egyptians. In most gardens and orchards in Ancient Rome, Priapus is found in the form of a statue in an intimidating pose, displaying a gigantic red phallus. His enormous genitals were a sign that brought fertility

A Greek terracotta Priapus, Hellenistic period 4th–3rd century BC; small stone statue of Priapus, Etruscan origin, 3rd–5th century BC; bronze dwarf with a giant phallus, Archaeological Museum, Naples, Italy; marble Priapus, Archaeological Museum, Ephesus, Turkey (left to right).

to everything that grew in the garden and at the same time warded off anything that could a danger: the evil eye, hungry birds or thieves. Priapus was worshipped as Bes in Asia Minor and later enjoyed great popularity in Ancient Greece. He was worshipped in particular in Lampsacus on the Hellespont, which is now the Turkish town of Lampsaki on the Dardanelles. In Greece, Priapus was regarded as the son of Dionysus and Aphrodite. When Aphrodite got pregnant, her mother Hera was jealous and placed her hands on Aphrodite's belly pronouncing a curse. As a result, Aphrodite gave birth to a misshapen dwarf with an enormous phallus.

The famous wall painting in the house of the Vetii in Pompeii depicts a man—perhaps Priapus himself—weighing his phallus in gold. Claudia Moser noted that: 'Priapus and his giant phallus represent three different kinds of prosperity: growth, represented by his enormous phallus; affluence, represented by the bag of coins which he holds and weighs; fertility, symbolized by the basket of fruit at his feet. The combination of money and the large member allowed the viewer to link the two, to equate the extensive quantity of each, an association evoked in the juxtaposition of the phallus and the bag of coins on the scale.'

Priapus figured more largely in Roman than in Greek art. Offerings of fruit and vegetables were placed by his statue and verses were often hung up near his statue. These poems were later called *Priapea*. Poets like Catullus, Horace, Martial and many other unknown poets wrote humorous and obscene verses in connection with Priapus.

The cult of the phallus did not have any important function in the official religion in Rome. Before Priapus was introduced in Rome, there was the cult of Mutinus Titinus or Mutunus Tutunus, who, until the first century BC was

Various Roman phallic objects, some like these tintinnabula (topmost) and amulets (bottom) are found all over Europe.

worshipped in a shrine located on Velian hill, in particular by young married women. Mutinus also played a part in ritual defloration at wedding feasts among the patrician class.

In addition to the worship of Priapus, the phallus enjoyed popularity in the form of phalluses or phallic objects (fascina) worn around the neck or around the belly as an amulet. These were worn to protect children from sickness, to ensure a propitious birth for pregnant women or victory for soldiers and generals. The phallus was called 'fascinum' in Latin, a term which clearly indicates its function as a protector against evil, since the verb fascinare means to cast a spell or to bewitch. These phallic objects were also worn to ward off impotence.

Pliny, in *Natural History* (28.4.7.), called it a 'medicus invidiae', a doctor or medicine for envy (invidia) or the evil eye.

This is also true of countless votive offerings and everyday objects, such as oil lamps and tintinnabulae. Tintinnabulae were bells in the shape of one or more phalluses, sometimes with different faces, which had special powers to ward off the evil eye. The function of these objects was not so much erotic as to provide magical protection. Phallic ex votos were offered to the gods for protection but also for male impotence and sexual diseases. Most of the offerings were in terracotta and are small with a narrow prepuce.

Etruscan votive in terracotta with a small prepuce (right) from Tarquina, Viterbo, Italy.

Other than evidence of the phallus in everyday life, it is clear that the phallus was not a source of shame for the Romans. When Augustus mockingly called the poet Horace 'purissimum penem' (my dear and most excellent penis), this is one more proof that for the

In the Roman Empire the phallus had a protective function. (Clockwise) Greco-Roman bronze figure of a comic actor with a theca; Roma terracotta comic figure with a big phallus; a phallus of painted tuff stone from Pompeii; phallus at a house in Pompeii; carved stone at remains of Chester's Roman Bridge, England; carved stone at Chester Roman fort; phallic symbol on a wall, Archaeological Museum Zadar, Croatia; phallic symbol on a wall in Sabratha, Libya; phallic carving Chester Roman fort, England.

Romans, the male genital was certainly not 'pudendum' or something to be ashamed of. Cerinthus (circa 100 AD) writes that people should not be ashamed of something that God himself created, and he was not ashamed of himself.

In theatres, the Romans played comedies where dwarfs and clowns with a big leather phallus, or theca, made the citizens laugh. In the city of Rome you could also find phallic drinking cups called phallivitroboli. Large phallic symbols were often carved on the Roman city gates and on the houses. They had the same protective function, warding off the evil eye and bringing health, happiness and good fortune to those who lived there and to the passing travellers.

The Greek messenger Hermes and his Roman counterpart Mercurius are often represented as ithyphallic figures. In Roman mythology, Hermes is also the inventor of fire by rubbing the male bar in the female excavation. During the spring festivals a big phallus, representing Hermes was carried through the streets

The phallus in Scandinavian and Celtic cultures

Scandinavia

Even after Scandinavia was converted to Christianity, the cult of the phallus worshipped by the indigenous people continued to play a role in its society. In the eleventh century, Adam, bishop of Bremen, described the heathen temple of Uppsala as containing images of the three major local gods: Odin (Wotan), Thor (Donar) and Frey (Freyr). The image of Frey had an enormous phallus: cum ingenti priapo. In the porch of the Romanesque church in Tommerby, Northern Jutland, Denmark, there is a granite phallus of 130cm high. This means that even two hundred years after the arrival of Christianity, a place could still be found for a phallic symbol in society.

A small bronze figure representing the god Freyr (left) and a granite phallus found in the porch of the Romanesque church in Denmark.

Nearly all wooden idols and figures from the Bronze and Ice Age disappeared and only some wooden objects were found preserved in swamps and moors—the Broddenbjerg man found in 1880 in Viborg, Denmark, a 55cm-long wooden phallus was excavated with a distinct glans in Jutland, Hedeliskaer Likewise, in the summer of 2002, Swedish archaeologists unearthed from the moors in Lunda near Strängnäs, three phallic figures that were dated between 460 and 600 AD.

Another proof of the phallic culture in Scandinavia are the *Edda*—a collection of old Scandinavian poems about mythological gods and heroes. One tale tells how the giant Thrym stole Thor's hammer, the phallic symbol of his power. As a ransom, Thrym asked the hand of Freya, the goddess of love. Thor, masqueraded as Freya, seized his hammer and slaughtered the giant, thereby regaining his phallic symbol.

The Celts

We can only conjecture about sexual and religious habits and morality in the confused times after the collapse of the Roman Empire. The Middle Ages are usually regarded as Christian, but while the first monks were arriving to convert Western Europe to Christianity, the Celts took over a number of Roman customs.

The giant of Cerne Abbas in Dorset, England, is cut in limestone and represents a Celtic man with a club in his right hand, and probably with a folded cloak in his left hand. Archaeologists believe him to be a local version of the Roma god, Hercules.

An example of this is the figure of Hercules cut into the chalk hillside of Cerne Abbas in Dorset, England. Michael Harrison, however, states that the name Cerne makes it clear whom this huge figure, cut out in the chalk is intended to represent: 'In the centuries, Cerne of Cerne has lost his horns but not—even through the era of Victorian public prudery—the unambiguous statement of his function as the Lord of the World's Fertility.'

Lia Fail, the Stone of Destiny, found on the hill of Tara near Dublin, Ireland.

Celtic society, like all patriarchal societies, had the cult of the penis at its core, to the extent that the human body itself was seen as a phallic object or symbol, and the severed head on a pillar a symbol of penis-power erected at strategic points on boundaries and at entrances. Lug, the potent male sky-god gave his name to strategic sites all over Europe: Lyon(s), Laon, London, Leyden, and perhaps Lucca—just as the Celts themselves gave their name enduringly to Galicia in Spain, Galicia in the Balkans, Wales, and, of course, Gaul. By this yardstick, the British Isles must once have been littered with phallic stones, pillars and carvings.

(Clockwise, left to right): The Abson man, fertility symbol on an exterior wall of the Church Saint Jones in Somerset, England; Exhibitionist corbel of a crude ithyphallic male drinker from Margam Abbey near Swansea, England; Celtic menhir near near Lochrist and Saint Uzec, Brittany, France, which were later changed into a Christian monument.

Sainte Geneviève gardant ses moutons *(St. Géneviève guarding her sheep), at Musée Carnavalet, Paris, France.*

The Celts, the Germans, the Gauls and the Visigoths already worshipped the cult of fertility before they were conquered and occupied by the Roman armies. In Britannia, the stone circle of Castlerigg was built as early as the Neolithic or Bronze Age (2500–1300 BC). The Roman Empire incorporated many cults which celebrated male energy. So, at one time, say near the end of the Roman period, Britain must have had rampant penises everywhere—from multi-phalliform lamps to marble herms, from low-reliefs of penises used as signs for and to brothels, to large menhirs, like Lia Fail, the Stone of destiny near Dublin in Ireland. Excavations of cult-figures of wooden warriors with large detachable quartzite penises, penis-and-vulva graffiti, phallic stones inside Cornish stone circles can be found on the British Islands dating back to the Bronze Age. More examples of Celtic influence in churches are found like the Abson Man crawling in megaphallic lust and the crude ithyphallic male from Margam Abbey near Swansea.

After the Romans, Christianity was imported into Western Europe and annexed the Celtic menhirs. Phallic loaves were blessed in church services to bring prosperity to the village and processions were organised in honour of the procreative organ. Since the church found it impossible to divert the people from their superstitious belief in the power of the stones to influence fertility and good and evil, the ecclesiastic authorities now attempted to turn pagan idols to Christian symbols, by implanting upon them the sign of the cross. There are many examples of this found in Brittany, France. In Paris, we can see a painting, dating back to the sixteenth century, of St. Genevieve, the patron saint of Paris, guarding her sheep in the middle of a circle of standing stones or menhirs. This is a clear evidence of a link between Christendom and earlier heathen rites.

An ordinance dating to the eighth century prescribes a sentence of several days on bread and water for worshipping a fascinum. The Church Council in Chelmsford issued an edict in the ninth century forbidding the practice of praying in front of a phallus. Although the Roman garden god was not explicitly invoked, his name was connected with phallic worship until the Middle Ages, or even later. Even the local clergy were sometimes influenced—in the thirteenth century, the pastor of Inverkeithing was summoned to appear before his bishop because he had organized a fertility dance around a phallic symbol in the churchyard during the Easter festival. He apparently gave an obscene performance by brandishing a wooden phallus and inciting the young girls gathered to licentious behaviour!

Medieval Europe

Antiquity promoted Priapus to a god,
The Middle Ages made him a saint
with different names.

—Richard Payne Knight, *The Worship of Priapus*

Phallic Saints!

The custom of hanging phalluses on the walls of buildings dates from Roman times but continued through the Middle Ages. These were found most frequently on the walls of churches, where they were thought to provide protection from all kinds of magic spells. The phallus protected both, the place where it was kept and all those who revered it or raised their eyes to it in faith. These phallic images were usually placed in the porch, as seen in the cathedral of Toulouse in France and a number of churches in the region of Bordeaux. However, during the French revolution, people turned on these phallic symbols and destroyed them as a symbol of the corruption of the clergy. But such phallic cults were generally opposed to Christianity, as Boudin relates in his *Etudes Anthropoligiques,* which tell how the inhabitants of Slavonia worshipped Priapus up to the twelfth century under the name of Pripegala.

In medieval times, sexuality was an open door leading to lust and uncontrolled passion. Sex was only permissible for the procreation of children—all other sexual motives were seen as mortal sin! In addition to the punishments in hell, it was also felt to be necessary to illustrate the sins themselves. Phalluses were sometimes displayed independently in churches, simply as a symbol of lust.

The codpiece was diffused all over Europe by the German and Swiss landsknechts.

After the Second World War, Professor Geoffrey Webb, secretary of the Royal Commission on Historical Monuments in England, was charged with drawing up a list of the damage suffered by English churches between 1939 and 1945.

Phallic images on Romanesque Christian churches. (Clockwise) a phallus in the church at Artaiz, Navarre, Spain; ithyphallic harp-player at the celebration of a carnival during which people display indecent postures; St. Christopher's Church, Courpiac, Gironde, France; circumcised ithyphallic Jew or Muslim, St. Peter's Church in Champagnolles, Charente Maritime, France; ithyphallic image with broken arms, Romanesque church at Givrezac, Charente-Maritimes, France; ithyphallic image in the Romanesque church in Saint-Palais, Gironde, France; the late Romanesque portal of the St. Stephen's cathedral in Vienna contains two phalluses on top of a double column.

To his amazement, he recorded the story of an altar that had been blown open during the bombing for the first time since the fourteenth century to reveal a... a huge phallus. In his final report, Webb wrote: ' ... that in 90% of all churches built since the Black Death in 1348 a God was placed in the altar. And what form did this old Giver of Life take? The form that is familiar to anyone who has ever visited a Hindu temple: the master symbol of the worldwide fertility cult – the universal phallus, through which all human life was made.'

Phallic saints like Saint Foutrin, the first bishop of Lyon in France, were also worshipped. His name was associated with the French verb, foutre which meant go to hell. Saint Guignolé, the first abbot of Landevenac, acquired his phallic attributes by the association of his name with the Latin verb 'gignere' (to beget). These saints were usually depicted with gigantic phalluses. When the Protestants captured Embrun in 1585, they discovered that the local people worshipped the phallus of Saint Foutrin and poured wine over it. And in 1562, when the Protestants razed the church in Orange, they found a large wooden phallus covered with leather.

In the description of the city of Antwerp, printed by Christopher Plantijn in 1596, Joannes Goropius Becanus writes that next door to the public prison, there was a small statue with a powerful magical influence, which was worshipped primarily by women who came to scrape off the powder on the phallus as a remedy for sterility. The statue was called Verpus in Antwerp, which is another name for Priapus. Later, it was transferred to the gate of the Steen, a former prison and came to be known as Semini—derived from semen—that indicates that it is a symbol of fertility.

Erotic insignia on medieval pilgrimages

In the late Middle Ages, between 1250–1550, pilgrimages were extremely popular all over Europe. St. James of Compostella in Galicia, Spain, was one of the most popular destinations. Pilgrims wore special insignia on their clothes or attached to their staff as it was believed that any one bearing such an insignia could count on protection and hospitality of the local people. They also protected the wearer from the evil eye and brought good luck: in other words these were amulets. These insignia were cheap mass-produced items cast in an alloy of tin and lead. Several thousands of them have been preserved over the centuries, or dug up by archeologists. They can be seen on a number of paintings by Hieronymus Bosch, and are also depicted on beggars, cripples and pilgrim cots in other art works dating back to the fifteenth and sixteenth centuries.

Votive insignia worn by pilgrims were often in the form of phallic creatures believed to protect the wearer from evil.

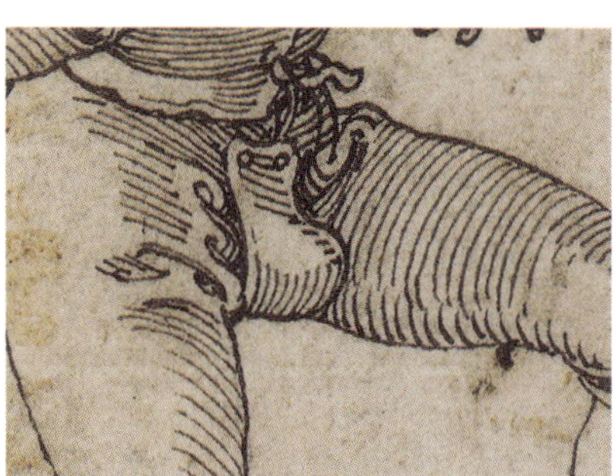

Nearly 50 per cent of all insignias or badges are pictures of saints or other religious subjects, but there are also other profane and above all erotica insignias that are frequently found—phalluses depicted as autonomous creatures of all kinds, with wings, arms and legs, claws, crowns, bells, peeping of trousers or even with a wheelbarrow. A.M. Koldeweij associates these stories with pilgrim's erotic insignias, which were often images of male and female genitalia represented as independent living creatures.

The codpiece: a sign of virility

The apparel oft proclaims the man
—William Shakespeare, *Hamlet* 1.3.

During the reign of Edward IV, (1461–83), the House of Commons obliged a man to wear a jacket or a long shirt, long enough 'to cover his private members and buttocks'.

At the end of the Middle Ages, men started to wear longer stockings and the idea came up to join the stocking at the upper part of the thighs and to put a triangular piece of cloth to cover the genitals. Later, this triangle became a kind of purse attached to the groin, first with a kind of a slide, later with laces, and was called la brayette or braguette in French, viseldeck in German and codpiece in English.

Codpieces (bottom left and above) were an integral part of mens' clothing in Europe during the Middle Ages.

After England's victory on the Burgundians in 1476, the codpiece was used all over Europe by the German and Swiss landsknechts. They attached a metal shell with a sponge at their coat of mail to protect their genitals. And in the *Thiers Livre, chap. VIII* by François Rabelais, there are extensive references to a piece of harness known as *'la braguette qui protège l'organe viril'*: the codpiece that protects the masculine organ. This new fashion was first taken over by farmers as shown in the paintings by Pieter Brueghel. Around 1,500 Italian soldiers were painted with oval codpieces. Later, in 1535 there came about bigger, convex and more pronounced codpieces as seen in painting of noble persons, kings and even Emperor Charles V from that period. As a piece of clothing, the codpiece draws attention towards the phallus, as well and signifies male characteristics like masculinity, political and military power.

During the reign of Charles V and Philips II codpieces were very popular in the Spanish court. If in England Elizabeth I had a great influence on women's dresses, from the other side of the Channel it was Henry III, the king of France,

The armour of Konrad von Bemelberg manufactured by Wolfgang Grossschedel and Ambrosius Gemlich Landshut, Germany, in 1535 (left). A German codpiece detail on an armour dating back to the sixteenth century.

that influenced men's fashion. With the disappearance of the codpiece, the overall costume showed a tendency towards feminization inspired by Henri III, accentuated by the small muffs carried and earrings worn. But there is also a medical explanation for the pronounced codpiece. Henry VII, as many of his contemporaries, suffered from syphilis and according to anthropologist Grace W. Vicary, the exaggerated codpieces contained medication to cure the disease. Dressings and ointments with mercury were put within the codpiece as a cure. In that view, the pronounced codpieces from that time were an adaptation of therapy to the first pandemic of syphilis in the beginning of the sixteenth century, rather than an expression of virility.

Later, with the advent of the Renaissance in western Europe, new phallus-related art came into being, brought over from Italy where the New Art and the Renaissance of Antiquity had already begun in the fifteenth century. Renaissance artists and philosophers considered the Romans as humans without shame that admired the naked body and praised sexuality. The Roman gods were powerful but not free of human feelings. They represented the human passions in a sublimated form. Venus and Priapus incarnated sexuality, and most gods and mythological figures had erotic adventures, both heterosexual or homosexual in nature. This resulted in a lot of erotical and sensual paintings and objects during Renaissance. Pornographic literature started with Pietro Aretino (1492–1556) in Italy and the most beautifully illustrated book of that time *Hypernerotomachia Poliphili* by Francesco Salviati (1510–63) shows an impressive woodcut of a phallus during the festivities of Dionysus. Even the famous artist Michelangelo's work showed this turn, as seen in this drawings of a veiled phallus. Roman

(Clockwise, left to right): Portraits of the Emperor Charles V by Jacob Seisenegger, 1532; Pier Maria Rossi di Sansecundo by Parmigianino; Ferdinand II, Archduke of Further Austria by Francesco Terzi; A young man, 1544, by Georg Penez; Antonio Navagero, 1565, by Giovanni Battista Moroni; and Guidobaldo II della Rovere by Agnola Bronzino.

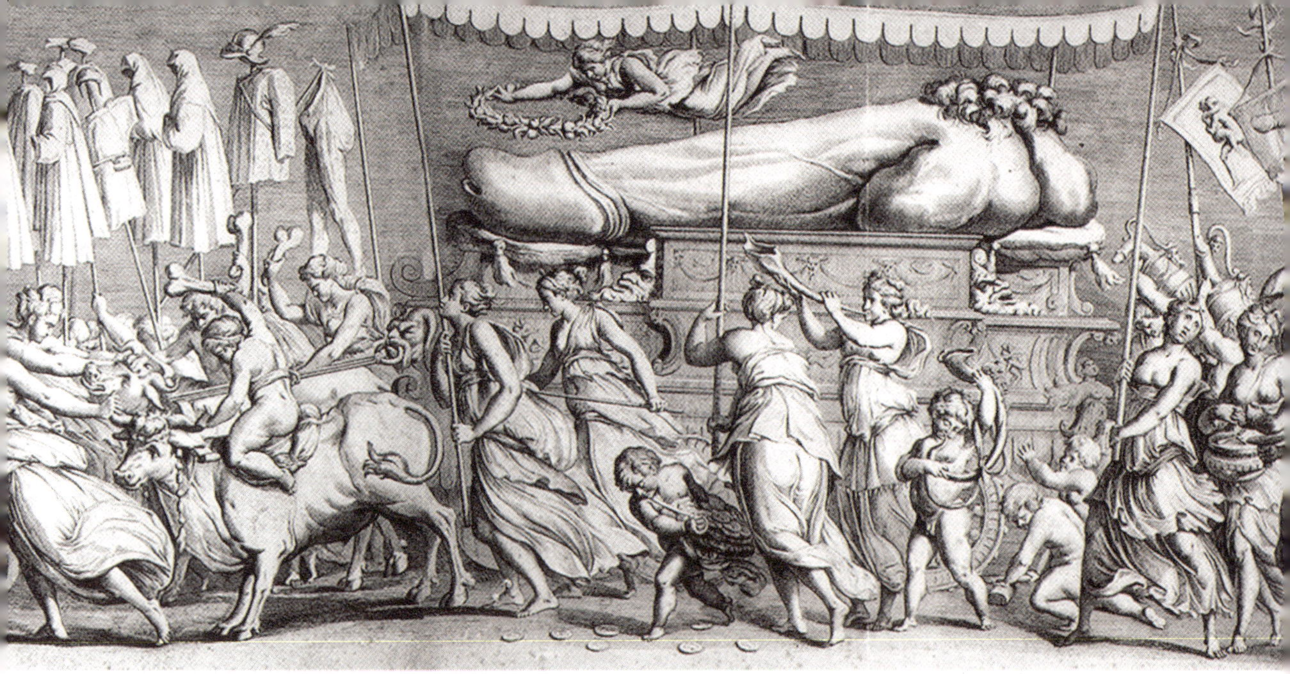

(Clockwise, left to right): Triumph of the Phallus *by Francesco Salviati;* Testa de Cazi *(head of penises) painted on a ceramic plate by Francisco Urbini; a Dutch painted phallus on a terracotta plate, ca.1400; a giant phallic decorative animal found at the cathedral at Ciudad Rodrigo, Spain; the sixteenth-century self-portrait of Michel Angelo, known as* Scherzo, *or the* Torments of the Flesh *(opposite).*

and early gothic churches used phalluses as decoration. Phallic objects during this time were not only used by the upper class but also in the lower middle class—many everyday objects like dishes and carafes were made in the form of a phallus.

Witches, male impotence, cats and phallic trees

Witches who collect twenty to thirty penises, put them in a bird's nest or a closed box, where they move as living limbs...

—Kramer, *Malleus Maleficarum*

Towards the end of the Middle Ages, sorcery and witchcraft replaced heresy as a focus of major concern. Many cultures worldwide continue to have widespread practices and cultural beliefs that are loosely translated into English as witchcraft, and these practices often occupy a religious, divinatory or medicinal role, often present within societies and groups whose cultural framework includes a magical world view.

In the Late Medieval and Renaissance times, the classic image of the witch flying in the air on a broom, preparing magic potions, and going through the open fire was relatively common. This tradition originates in the pagan feminine mystery rites concerning marriages and birth, where a broomstick would play an important part. In Rome, the broom was the symbol of a priest–midwife, and of Hecate, the goddess who also presided over marriage, and the broom symbolized sexual union. The connection with the phallus is of course obvious, riding the broomstick signifying the sexual position where the woman is on top, a position considered by the medieval Church to be a perversion. The broomstick was anointed with what was called flying ointment—probably aconite or a mixture of hallucinogenic substances such as hemlock, mandrake and belladonna. The ointment smeared on the handle of a broom would then be straddled so that it could be absorbed by the sweat glands around the genitals and anus. It is striking that the witch is often portrayed naked and sits astride on the broom clamped between her 'labiae'. To ride, at that time, also had sexual connotation of intercourse, as can be seen in an etching by Francesco Parmigianino, dating back to 1530, in which an old witch is riding on a gigantic phallus with a staff under her arm like a lance. Dominating the male member symbolizes domination of the male social position and power.

Witches by Hans Baldung Grien, dated 1508.

Despite the archetypal image of a folkloric witch as an ugly old woman, a witch is also associated with sex. In manuscripts dating back to the sixteenth century, the persecuted witch always had sex with the devil or one of his worshippers during the Black Sabbath. The witch is mostly represented naked in prints and paintings, and everywhere there is a direct association between witches and sexuality. She rides the hedge or penis, or demon by disposing of the virile power of men. She can summon this virile power herself or can steal it from men by egressing her body. Going off into a trance she creates a pure spirit leaving her body.

Witches and phalluses were a common theme in art during this time; like this sixteenth-century painting, Saul and the Witch of Endor *by Jacob van Oostsanen (right) and* Meeting of Witches *by Urs Graf 1514 (below).*

Cats and stolen phalluses

In the late medieval times, several images and decorations depict images of genitals as live creatures. In 2008, Renilde Vervoort mentions several illustrations of cats holding a phallus in their muzzle. She suggests that these cats symbolized the devil or a witch who transformed herself into a cat. Cats, as transformed witches, were considered to be capable of attacking the male sex since they are alert at night and can see in the darkness. Cats were also regarded as capable of stealing the penises of men who had illicit sexual adventures—stories covered extensively in *Witches and Sex, Cats and Stolen Phalluses in Medieval and Renaissance Europe*. In many pictures and tales the cat is a faithful ally of the witch. Cats are present in different paintings representing witches in erotic situations. In a drawing by Hans Baldung Grien we see a cat in the bottom right corner. The witch on the right rides a forked stick, her long hair waving in the wind, a

Sepulchrũ
Samuelis

sign of sexual lust. Behind her, is a putto holding the witch and an older witch on her right side, who is seen touching a firm penis on the stick. The witch on the right clamps the stick between her legs with two phalluses on the same stick. The witch sitting in the foreground carries a long straight candle in her left hand, suggesting a penis and lights the candle by a fart.

In the *Exempla*, the cat was a symbol of the vain and of voluptuous woman. Prostitutes and women looking for sex were compared with cats because of their instincts. In fact, the sexual connotation between cats and women persists still today in the word 'pussy' (Dutch: poesje; Italian micia; French chatte, German: muschi).

The idea of losing one's penis, was one of the absolute biggest fears in medieval society in Europe. And the cause of such a disaster was often thought to be witchcraft. This fear and concept came from the belief of the phallus being a symbol of virility, male power, and a representation of male domination in the society. And so, fits the image of the sexually insatiable witches as bossy women that could take over men's power.

In various illustrations and art pieces through history, one can see images of witches either roasting or draping the phalluses over sticks like sausages, a connotation belonging to the world of carnival, inversing the moral order—just like in a painting from 1526, *Saul and the witch of Endor* by Jacob Cornelisz van Oostsanen in which the witches roast sausages. For instance, in a woodcut piece, from 1508, by Hans Baldung Grien, there are five witches with their legs suggestively spread and nude, doing magic work. The flying witch in the picture with long hair and open legs is sitting back to front on a goat— riding backwards, being nude with loose hair suggests a rampant sexual desire and lustful impudence! While the witch on the left raises a drinking cup and beneath her arm we can see three sausages (phalluses!) on a stick.

This mural, discovered in 2000 in Massa Marittima, Tuscany, Italy, dates back to the late thirteenth century. The phallus tree bears 'phallus fruits' which are disproportionately large, mainly erect and complete with scrotal sacs. Under the tree stand eight witches.

The phallic tree

In the year 2000, an exceptional mural was discovered behind the plaster of Fonte Nuova fountain. This mural found in the medieval town of Massa Marittima in Tuscany, Italy, dates back to 1265. The dominant image of this large mural—six metres wide and five metres high—is a tree set against a pale background. But the tree portrayed carried exceptional fruits—phalluses distributed across all the branches, disproportionately large with a scrotum and clearly in an aroused state.

After this discovery, there were several more discoveries made. By 2010, eight more medieval illustrations with phallus trees were found. There is definitely a link between the phallus, fountains and fertility; certainly in Italy. Sculptured phalluses can be found on the Fonte di Pescaia in Siena and on the fountains in San Gimigiano. Though, it can also be that most phallus trees find their roots in the link between infertility and impotence on the one hand and sorcery and witchcraft on the other.

Forbidden and taboo: the anti-phallic culture

The parts the Greeks called sacred have been rebaptised 'shameful' by the Christians.

—Hervé Bazin, *Abécédaire*

It might be surprising that an eminently human phenomena like sexuality and worshipping of the phallus, which are found all over the world, should disappear completely in Europe from the sixteenth century onwards. Culture and morality of the urbanized bourgeoisie changed drastically between the fifteenth and twentieth century. Sexuality was relegated in the background, while the moral façade behind which citizens hid, became more and more important. Sex became a social taboo and it was forbidden to display human genitals. All places where such motifs would be were painted over or covered with a fig leaf. In 1564, Pope Paulus V commissioned Daniele da Volterra, a disciple of Michelangelo, to cover all nudes of the Judgement Day in the Sistine chapel. This caused much mirth

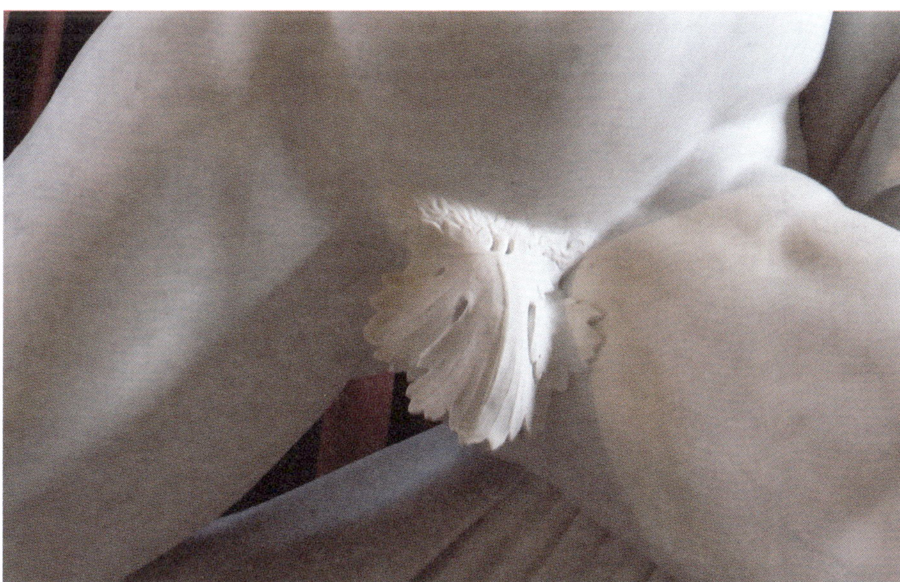

(Right) A detail from Theseus and the Centaur, carved in marble by Antonio Canova. A phallic caricature of Pope Julius II (left) by Jacques Callot for Rabelais' book Songes drolatiques de Pantagruel.

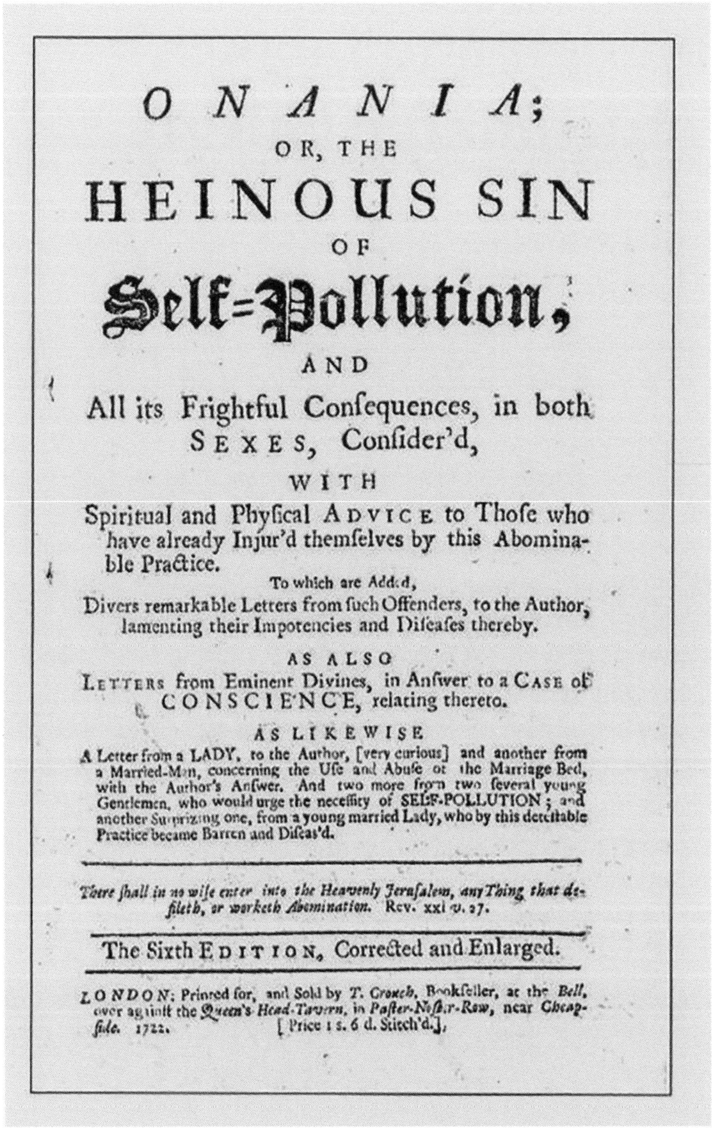

ONANIA;
OR, THE
HEINOUS SIN
OF
Self-Pollution,
AND
All its Frightful Confequences, in both SEXES, Confider'd,
WITH
Spiritual and Phyfical ADVICE to Thofe who have already Injur'd themfelves by this Abominable Practice.
To which are Added,
Divers remarkable Letters from fuch Offenders, to the Author, lamenting their Impotencies and Difeafes thereby.
AS ALSO
LETTERS from Eminent Divines, in Anfwer to a CASE of CONSCIENCE, relating thereto.
AS LIKEWISE
A Letter from a LADY, to the Author, [very curious] and another from a Married-Man, concerning the Ufe and Abufe of the Marriage Bed, with the Author's Anfwer. And two more from two feveral young Gentlemen, who would urge the neceffity of SELF-POLLUTION; and another Surprizing one, from a young married Lady, who by this deteftable Practice became Barren and Difeas'd.

There fhall in no wife enter into the Heavenly Jerufalem, any Thing that defileth, or worketh Abomination. Rev. xxi v. 27.

The Sixth EDITION, Corrected and Enlarged.

LONDON: Printed for, and Sold by *T. Crouch*, Bookfeller, at the *Bell*, over againft the *Queen's Head-Tavern*, in *Pafter-Nofter-Row*, near *Cheapfide*. 1722. [Price 1 s. 6 d. Stitch'd.]

among his fellow painters who nicknamed him 'Il Braghettone' or the purveyor of trousers! We only find the phallus depicted sporadically during that period—in satirical pictures like those drawn by Jacques Callot (1592–1635) for Rabelais' *Songes drolatiques de Pantagruel*, in which he immortalizes both Pope Julius II and the French king François I in a phallic caricature.

There are several reasons why this transition to an anti-phallic culture spread all over Europe. The church fathers had a fundamental role in Christian morality.

Onania; or the Heinous sin of Self Pollution, *edited in London in 1722 (left) and frontispiece of the French edition of the book on all diseases produced by M. Tissot in 1774 (right).*

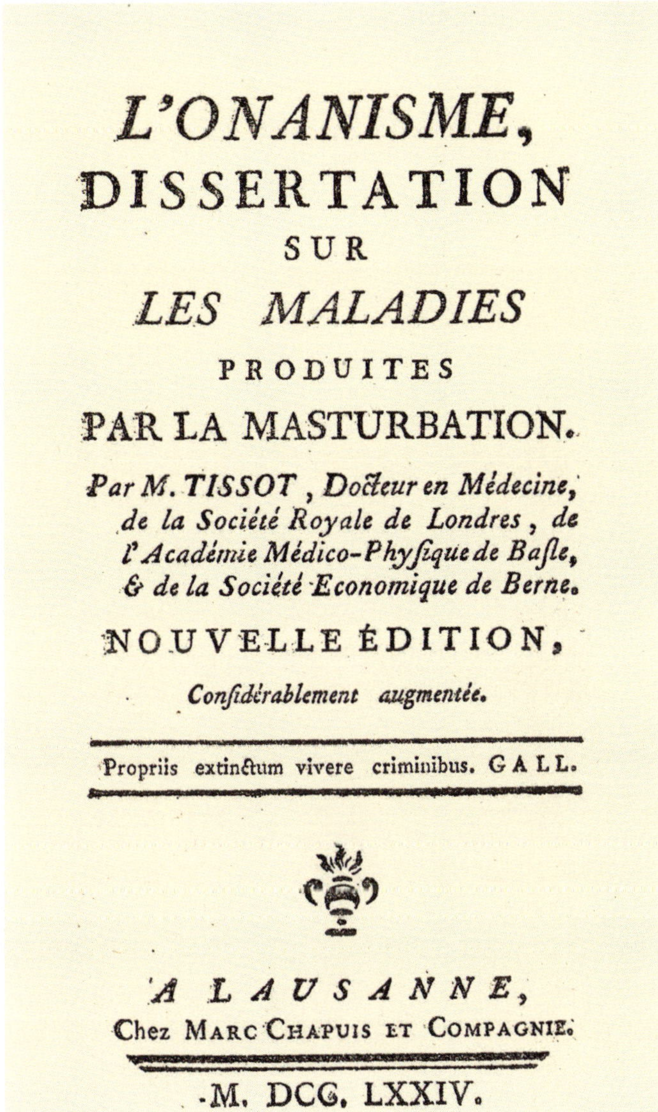

L'ONANISME,
DISSERTATION
SUR
LES MALADIES
PRODUITES
PAR LA MASTURBATION.

Par M. TISSOT, Docteur en Médecine, de la Société Royale de Londres, de l'Académie Médico-Physique de Basle, & de la Société Economique de Berne.

NOUVELLE ÉDITION,
Considérablement augmentée.

Propriis extinctum vivere criminibus. GALL.

A LAUSANNE,
Chez MARC CHAPUIS ET COMPAGNIE.
M. DCC. LXXIV.

Saint Augustine called sexuality 'revoltant', Saint Arnobius called it 'dirty and humiliating', Saint Methodius called sex as 'inappropriate', Saint Jerome 'indecent' and Tertullian 'improper'. A big part of this change was due to the Christian morality brought on by the Reformation and the Contra-Reformation. All these negative elements were accentuated during the Reformation by Martin Luther (1483–1546) and Johannes Calvin (1509–1564), and in a reaction the Catholic Church of Rome reacted with an even more severe Contra-Reformation that lead to the foundation of the Jesuit Order, the Inquisition and the Index of forbidden books.

At the same time, there was a rise in medical science studies that attributed all neurological diseases to masturbation. Anti-phallic culture reached its peak from 1722 onwards, following the first medical publication on the subject in England, which outlined three basic ideas: the heinous sin, abominable practice and its frightful consequences.

Another even more influential publication was that of the Swiss physician Samuel Auguste Tissot, which first appeared in Latin in 1758, and later in 1760 in French, titled *L'Onanisme, dissertation sur les Maladies produites par la Masturbation.* As a medical doctor, Tissot set off a general psychosis among people through fear of all the illnesses said to be caused by masturbation or self-pollution.

In addition, educational theorists, at the end of the eighteenth century, accepted Tissot's theories and opinions without questions and applied them rigorously to the education of the young. It was then that the most radical measure against masturbation among boys was infibulation—in 1887, Dr Milton recommended different types of iron rings with sharp spikes to be placed over the penis as a remedy. Later, a variety of special belts and contraptions replaced this painful operation. Finally, the fear of venereal diseases loomed all over Europe since the first pandemic of syphilis after the siege of Naples in 1496. Big publicity panels placed in all public places warned against venereal diseases and the most effective method, before antibiotics, was to avoid intercourse.

In conclusion, sex—and also the phallus—was viewed as the potential cause of many disorders: venereal diseases, mental degeneration and moral depravation, and also poverty. In the eyes of the moralist, the economist and the political philosopher, it is not proper for the poor to beget more children than they can afford to raise. Sexual excesses and misbehaviour are the main causes of the conditions of the inhabitants of the slums and a great number of philanthropists embark on moralizing the urban proletariat. But the aristocracy remained out of the focus! The whole society was caught in a dialectical contradiction of the natural, very similar to the one that Freud will describe in individuals a few years later.

From all this, it is clear that by the end of the nineteenth century, so little was left of the old phallic culture or reverence of the phallus that one could call it the century of the anti-phallus culture.

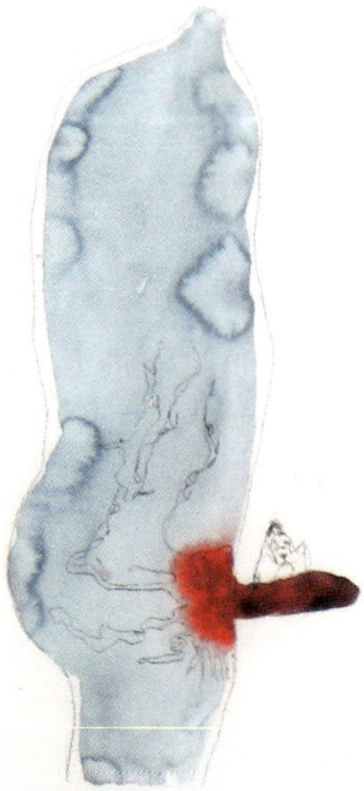

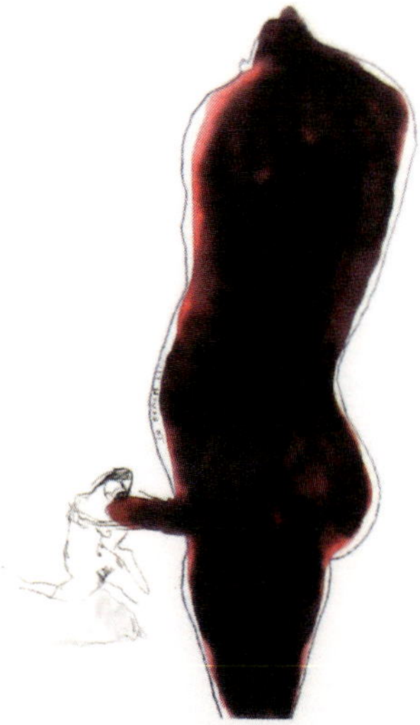

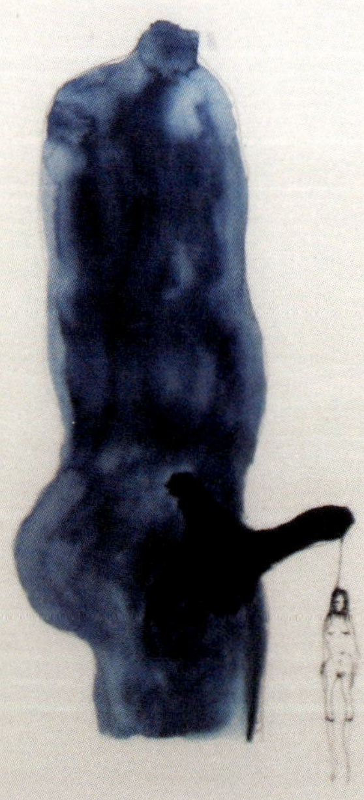

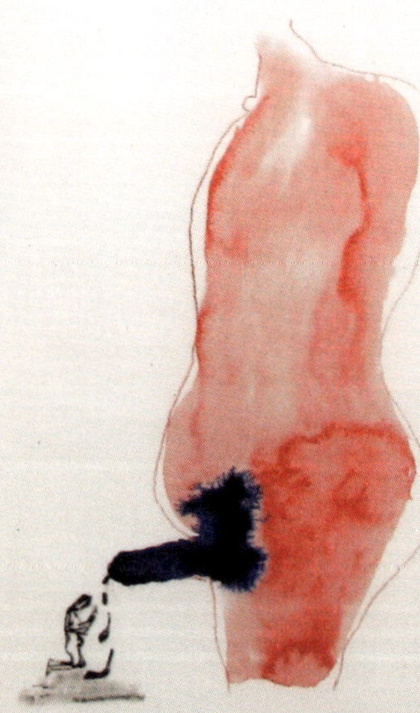

The phallus in erotic and modern art

It is time to fly in the face of saint Augustine, that accomplished castrator of his own libido and militant campaigner against the body and the world of pleasure. Now with the new Catechism of the Catholic Church, it is time to affirm the innocence of eroticism and the genius of Eros, who gives the soul a body and sexuality its sublime dimension...

—Jacques Sojcher, *Eros Sublime*

Erotic art

During the anti-phallic centuries, sexuality and sex did not disappear but were suppressed and pushed aside. The opulent and naked painted women in Renaissance art are well-known, but they did respond to biblical or mythological themes. This resulted in a lot of erotic and sensual paintings and objects during the Renaissance. A moral decline appeared in Europe with the French Revolution, followed by the advent of the Libertines. After 1900, just like phallic culture disappeared sixteenth century onwards and made way for an anti-phallic culture, later various new causes and influences came to bear which made sexuality more free and open again.

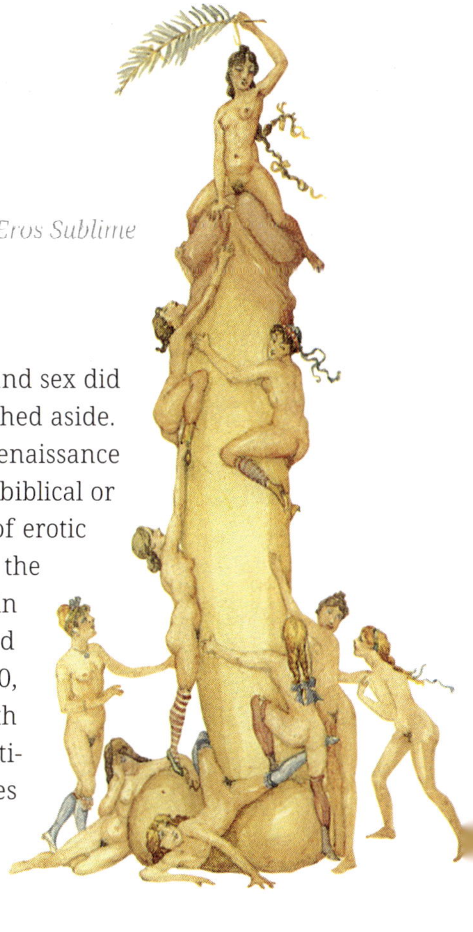

Many erotic drawings were published anonymously like the The Big Stake *(right), which was published in the Netherlands around 1900. Very daring for its time! Another like* Do not Abandon Me *is a painting by Louise Bourgeois (1911-2010) and Tracey Emin (1963-).*

Erotic prints drawn by Borel, engraved by Elluin and published clandestinely in London, were notorious.

The penis and phallus both emerged from the shadow and the taboo placed on them in the nineteenth and twentieth centuries. But the phallus never regained the wider significance of fertility and religious symbol, nor any kind of phallic worship revived, and the phallus only held erotic and sexual significance.

Erotic literature and pornography became a popular genre, but most artists, like the illustrator of Pierre Louÿs' book *Three Daughters of their Mother*, did not dare to make themselves known. Erotically-illustrated books were printed underground and illegally, anonymous or with a pseudonym. Most were censured and confiscated at publication and enclosed in the Private Case of the British Library in London or *L'Enfer* (the Hell) of the Bibliothèque Nationale in Paris or Der Giftschrank (the Poison cabinet) in Germany and Austria. In libraries, the word erotica was replaced by curiosa!

Poets such as Paul Verlaine (1844–96), Arthur Rimbaud (1851–91), Frédéric Bataille (1850–1918) and many others in France published erotic poems in accompanied with erotic drawings. The drawings which Eugène de Poitevin made for *The Three of Life*, published in 1832, were extremely daring for that time.

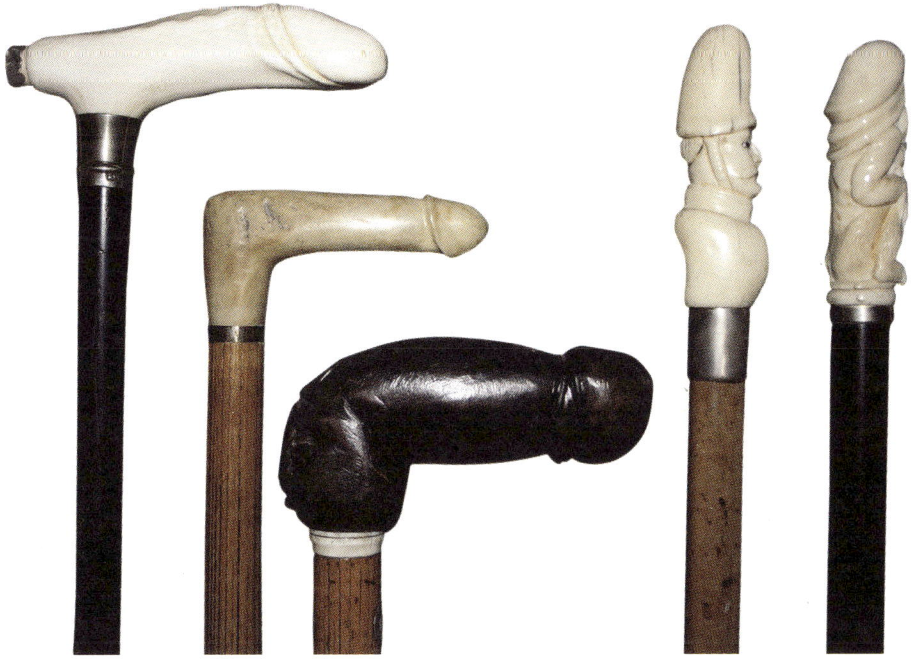

The shape of the phallus was incorporated into many everyday objects like English ivory snuff bottles (top, left), Japanese ivory paperweights with shibayama inlay, and walking sticks with phallic shaped handles.

Satire often combined phallic allusions with larger narratives. A late-nineteenth century Art Nouveau style illustration by Aubrey Beardsley which showed the Lacedaemonian ambassadors and The Examination of the Herald *with giant phalluses (left). Belgian artist, Félicien Rops' satirical cartoon of the French king Louis XIV with an enormous phallus (right) with the caption: Tout est grand chez les Roys (Everything is on a grand scale with kings!).*

Meanwhile, phallic-erotic objects like snuffboxes, walking sticks and corkscrews were being made for the dandy bourgeoisie. At the end of the nineteenth century, there was even a booming industry of Japanese shibayama (the inlay of a design with shells and coral into an ivory) which produced erotic objects for the British aristocracy.

Eroticism came more and more into the foreground in Western culture. Jacques Sojcher writes: 'Eroticism is without doubt a sublimation of sexuality, propelled by the power of the sexual urge. This projection or transposition extends sexuality into the realm of the non-sexual, and eroticizes all the senses, all feelings and thoughts.'

Jugendstil and Art Nouveau emerged around the turn of the century in Western Culture. In 1896, Aubrey Beardsley illustrated *The Lacedaemonian Ambassadors* and *The Examination of the Herald* with erotic drawings with giant phalluses in the characteristic Art Nouveau style. The Belgian artist, Felicien Rops produced a great number of phallic drawings, including a satirical cartoon of the French king Louis XIV with an enormous phallus with the caption '*Tout est grand chez les Roys*', which translates as 'everything is on a grand scale with kings!'

Man Ray's 1920 exhibit Presse-papiers à Priape, *Keith Haring's provocative drawing (center) and* Princess X, *by Constantin Brancusi, polished bronze and limestone block (right).*

Modern art

Modern art was looking for new directions, forms and expressions. For the first time it was also an expression of contestation and protest. At the beginning of the twentieth century, the intense sensuality of the paintings of Egon Schiele (1890–1918), a protégé of Gustav Klimt, was regarded as decadent and pornographic. Later, modern art came to be one that was no longer expected to be beautiful, its primary function was to shock! And the phallus served this purpose by being depicted primarily in a satirical, humorous or shocking guise.

Constantin Brancusi (1876–1957) ached with relentless persistence to achieve and convey the pure essence of things. In 1915–16, he created *Princess X*—such a revelation of its supposed obscenity that it prompted the work's instant removal from the *Salon des Indépendants* in 1920, leaving Brancusi incensed by the audience's apparent imperceptions. But Brancusi replied, 'What is real is not the external form, but the essence of things ... it is impossible for anyone to express anything essentially real by imitating its exterior surface.'

There is no denying the headstrong cockiness this erect form presents. No denying the geometric suggestion of a chap and its chums. As Brancusi clarified, it was not a lewd anatomical vulgarity, but rather, a critical impression of the wealthy French psychoanalyst and author, Princess Marie Bonaparte, great-grand niece of Emperor Napoleon the First, and figure of great distaste to the modest Romanian craftsman. Instead, the artists claimed his *Princess X* a symbol of feminine temperament—a busty dame with an elongated neck.

(Clockwise, left to right): A gnome with a phallus by Paul Mc Carthy, Winter Pissing *by Gilbert & George, erotic comic art by Jean Yves Mitton, painting by American pop artists Tom Wesselman and* Plat de Bites *by French artist Cesar.*

In 1920, Man Ray exhibited his *Presse-papiers à Priape* in the USA. Giorgio de Chirico's *Painting with Cannons* is also intended to be provocative and the drawings of Keith Haring are purposely aggressive and shocking.

Many artists of the second half of the twentieth century and the twenty-first century did not have any inhibitions depicting phalluses in their work, Pablo Picasso (1881–73) being an excellent example. So are French artist César Baldacinni (1921–98) with his *Plat de Bites* in 1979 and the American pop art artist Tom Wesselman in his *Bedroom Painting*. Both found their inspiration in the phallus, but purely in artistic terms and not for its symbolic meaning. Allen Jones and Wesselman, as the representants of pop art, take sexuality as their theme and as the leitmotif of a new society with a desire for sexual emancipation.

After 1950, it became normal to find art galleries displaying sexually provocative and even obscene works of art. Paul McCarthy (1945) is focused on sex and aggression and critiques the way of violence in the world. Louise Bourgeois also sculpted and painted phalluses in her work. In 1991, Gilbert & George painted pissing penises in London as an expression of their homoerotic relation.

Another aspect of art in the twentieth century is the development of photography and the cartoon comic. In the field of photography, Robert Mappelthorpe is the most known name for his portraits of male nudes and genitals. Alain D'Hooghe writes: 'Through photography eroticism attains an unedited physiological verity. In achieving this, the photographer is balancing on the thin line between eroticism and pornography.'

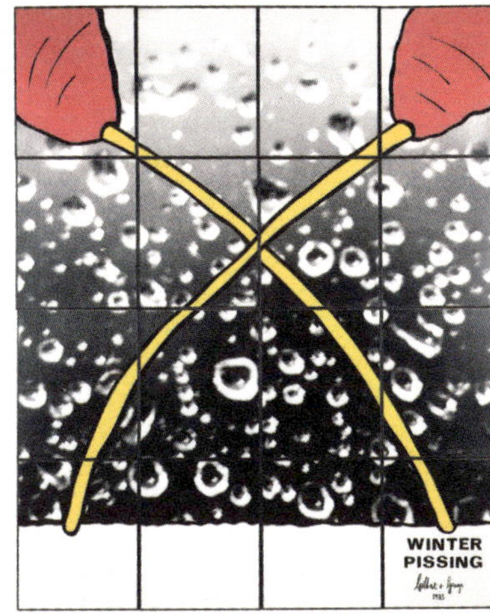
WINTER
PISSING

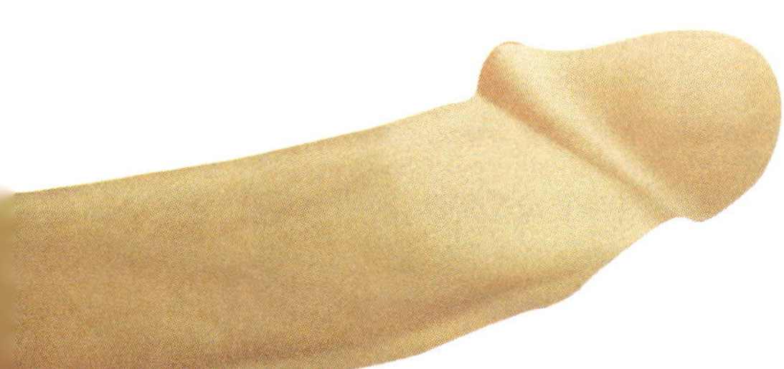

The collection of phallic amulets of Sigmund Freud, found at the Sigmund Freud Museum, London.

Finally, sexuality and eroticism have turned up in the world of the strip cartoons. Artists such as Jean Yves Mitton, Schuiten, Erich von Gota, Serpieri, Milo Manara, Hanz Kovacq and Jacovitti have won international fame in this field. But again, this is all primarily erotic material, bordering on pornography without any deeper symbolism. As Paolo Leonardi says: 'The comic strip has not escaped the phenomenon of eroticism. Specialized comic strips have emerged and today certain authors even go so far to plunge the reader into the world of pornography.' In France and Belgium, *Nathalie, la petite hôtesse* (Nathalie, the little air hostess) by Joop de Boer and Jaap van Linden and *L'érection* (The Erection) by Lounis Chabane and Jim became collector's items.

While art has done much to put the spotlight back on sexuality and the phallus over the last decades, psychiatry has also played a very important role. Each on the basis of their own premises, Freud, Jung and Lacan all emphasized the symbolic nature of the phallus. In a letter to Jung, dated 11 November 1909, Freud described the Vestal Virgins as brides of the penis. This indicates that Freud was well aware of the phallic symbolism of the Roman world. In fact, the father of modern psychology gathered together a collection of phallic amulets during his life and this collection can still be seen at the Freud Museum in London.

POWER AND ECSTASY: THE CULT OF THE LINGAM

Alka Pande

Is the phallus/linga pha(bu)llus/fabulous?

Whoever lives his life without honouring the lingam is truly poor, sinful and without luck. To honour this giver of joy is worth more than good works, fasting, pilgrimages, sacrifices and other virtues.

—Shiva Purana, *Shiva: The Wild God of Power and Ecstasy*

Tracing the story and evolution of the linga and dipping into the re-telling of the many myths and Puranic tales in Hindu tradition, show the linga becoming a potion of magic, fertility, procreation, vitality and inhibited continuous pleasure. The well spring of lust, desire and culmination of love and longing, the penis is both an emblem of power and pleasure. In that sense, the phallus is perceived very differently in Hindu mythology and culture as opposed to the Judeo-Christian religion, where sex and pleasure are antonyms. In ancient Hindu culture, the phallus then becomes the most important tool of carnal pleasure. According to one story, when Kamadeva, the god of love, disturbed Shiva's meditation trance so he falls in love with Parvati, such was Shiva's fury that he punished Kamadeva by giving him marks of a vagina on his face! In the same sacred landscape, there is a story which has a detailed description of the sexual act between two male Gods, Shiva and Vishnu, that led to the birth of their son Ayyappa, the celibate god. This can only happen in the religious culture of India where every god has a wife and primordial gods like Shiva and Parvati are known for their passionate lovemaking.

Women praying to a shivalingam in this folio from the Ragmala series.

Shiva, the god, symbolized by the linga in India, figures in many stories related to the erotic in texts. In one of the versions, the *Kamasutra* first came into being as Nandin recited it while he was overhearing the sounds of Shiva and Parvati's lovemaking. According to the scripture, 'While the Great God Shiva was experiencing the pleasures of union with his wife Uma for a thousand years as

A relief from the Virupaksha temple.

the gods count them, Nandin went to guard the door of their sleeping chamber and composed the *Kamasutra*.' In the last chapter of the *Kamasutra*, aphrodisiacs and techniques are outlined which are believed to strengthen the phallus.

Shiva, being an ancient, primeval god, is mentioned in the Vedas as Rudra, as Pashupati—the lord of animals—in Indus Valley seals and seen extensively in wayside shrines all over India as votive offerings of snake stones. In the *Kamasutra*, Shiva is represented as the linga, the marker of male identity. Sir Richard Burton and Foster Fitzgerald Arbuthnot, the two translators of the text, did this to bring more acceptability to the text as it was considered erotic by Victorian scholars.

The linga brought in the spiritual into the erotic aspect of the *Kamasutra*, extending into the mainstream retelling of the text. This meeting of the erotic and the spiritual is widely seen in artistic interpretations and representations on medieval temples found at sites like Khajuraho, Konarak and Modhera, to name a few. These temples and structures are full of amorous couples in 'mithuna' or having coital sex , where the male erect penis is not an uncommon sight. The famous Khajuraho temples, built between 950 and 1050 CE, carry carvings that highlight the sexual union between the different Indian gods and goddesses. These carvings suggest that the temples were not only for performance of prayers but also a place where the four purushartha or the four aims of human life according to Hindu philosophy: dharma (righteousness), artha (monetary value), kama (desire) and moksha (salvation) were taught. Be it literature, poetry, popular culture, or simple way side shrines, the phallus is vital is every aspect of life in India.

Due to being such an important part of everyday life, the phallus has led to the erection of many stories, myths, legends and devotion around it. The myths around it are most connected to Shiva—to understand this, it is perhaps important to understand the story that involves the three gods of the Hindu trinity, Vishnu, Brahma and Shiva. According to that Brahma and Vishnu were once quarrelling over who was the supreme god. Brahma claimed he was the Creator and hence

Ruins at the Baleshwar Shiva temple at Chhattisgarh.

supreme, while Vishnu claimed he was superior as he was both the Creator and the Destroyer. Just then, Shiva's voice sounded from within a pillar ablaze with light, declaring that he was pre-eminent as he was the Creator, the Preserver and the Destroyer. Astonished, Brahma and Vishnu put aside their quarrel and journeyed in opposite directions to ascertain the size of the lingam—the pillar of light. The *Linga Purana* posits that the lingam is rooted in the formless and the non-manifested. Therefore, Shiva is himself without the lingam. It belongs to Shiva and the one who possesses it is the Supreme Being. In that sense, the phallus is the foundation of the whole world; everything issues from it.

The shivalingam in a square star-shaped garbha griya found at the 5th–7th century Shiva temple at Sirpur, Chhattisgarh.

The lingam, known more as a shivalingam, is a specific icon of the Hindus and has its own unique representations. Shaivism—the strand of Hinduism that worships Shiva—is an important sect and the phallic symbol of the lingam is a constant icon which is a permanent feature in Shaivism and its regional representations.

A. Danielou in *Gods of Love and Ecstasy: The Traditions of Shiva and Dionysus*, translates from the *Shiva Purana*, 'I am not distinct from the phallus. The phallus is identical with me. It draws my faithful to me. Therefore,

The famous Madurai temple.

it must be worshipped. My well-beloved! Wherever an upright male organ is to be found, I myself am present even if there is no other representation of me.'

The lingam/penis/phallus/ becomes an important 'member' of pleasure, desire and seed-giver. And since it is a symbol of Shiva, it is a stronger part of his identity and icon of worship, reverence, fertility, vitality and energy.

The phallus plays a dual role as the organ of procreation and the bringer of 'ananda' or divine ecstasy, which comes about from the union of the lingam/ phallus and the yoni/vulva. Pleasure and desire are manifested through the phallus. The vulva and the phallus, as well as the bodily fluids, were considered essential in the fertility rites within tantric philosophy. In this philosophy, the ananda ultimately gives way to detachment and enlightenment. In some tantric sects, the shivalingam is depicted as a phallic symbol and the base as a vulva, or yoni. While the lingam represents the ubiquitous or static absolute, the yoni represents the dynamic, creative energy of God, the womb of the universe. This touching of the lingam and yoni has its own unique ramifications. It also throws light on the way the cult of the lingam is understood, expressed, explored, worshipped and used as a metaphor in popular imagination. In Hinduism, the yoni is the emblem of the feminine cosmic creativity (Shakti), the highest symbol of Devi, who is also the consort of Shiva. Symbolizing this union, Shaivite temples have a circular yoni pedestal for the lingam. This ancient Hindu interpretation of the linga and yoni is entirely metaphysical and psychological.

Clearly, the lingam—be it in a sculpture or painting—is viewed as a metaphor and motif for the primordial god Shiva in all his forms—as Rudra (Lord of wind), Mahakaal (Lord of all times) Nataraja (King of the art of dancing), Ardhanarishvara (Androgynous form of Shiva and Parvati), Hari Hara (Remover of sins and the Destroyer) and Somesvara (Lord of all).

Shiva has been worshipped in the form of the lingam by women for centuries in India, as seen in this folio painting.

References to the phallic cult are found across the subcontinent and especially in south India. The first ithyphallic symbol dates back to the Indus Valley civilization. Danielou speaks of how the 'rough and courageous Aryans discovered a marvellous civilization in India—cities of gold and silver with splendid palaces and incalculable riches, offering every pleasure. These cities were inhabited by a dark-skinned people, who worshipped the phallus and the snake and who fought bravely against the invader.' The phallus was not mentioned in Vedic writings and the Aryans seemed unaware of the concept. There is, however, a reference to the Shishnadva, or the phallic god in the Rig Veda. His worship was banned due to the socio-cultural mores that prevailed then, probably because the phallus was associated with pagan cults that incorporated black magic and sorcery in their worship rituals. The revival of Shaivism in the second century BCE redefined these attitudes towards the phallus in Vedic texts.

Throughout the book, the phallus has been examined, studied, collected and celebrated from different cultures across the world. The phallus, therefore, becomes necessary and relevant at this point for me and to address the question which is raised in every readers' mind—why am I returning to the religious icon of Shiva after investigating the phallus artistically, culturally and sociologically? After the exploration of the phallus from the past chapters, this one views it as a cultural construct invested with sexuality, fertility and having cultural ramifications, especially in context of the South Asian subcontinent. Having said that, the lingam lends itself to multiple interpretations and myths throughout history and time. As an art historian, I am picking strands that my study has taken me to. Throughout history and literature, the phallus has been mentioned as lingam and linga interchangeably—something I will be following in this chapter.

Emergence of the lingam

'The *linga* is an oblong shaped object worshipped by Hindus around the world as a symbol of Lord Shiva, the God of Transformation, who is beyond all forms. The circularity of the *linga* represents the endless, all-pervasiveness of Divinity.'

—Mat McDermott

Indian cultural traditions, particularly those related to Hindu gods and goddesses, abound with innumerable stories both in the 'margi', or high culture and the 'lokdharmi', or popular culture. And Shiva is regarded the first amongst the holy trinity of the primordial gods, his lingam becomes the object of greatest sanctity, even more, sacred than any anthropomorphic in that age, as stated by Stella Kramrisch, a leading art historian and a specialist on India art.

In fact, the shivalingam is the most emphatic icon of Shiva. The beginnings of the shivalingam go back to the Indus Valley civilization, the first physical representation of the powerful erect penis which is also known as the urdhavalingam—a symbol of active procreation and Shiva's potent, fiery and fecund semen. However, the very concept of Shiva goes even further back.

From the Puranic period onwards, be it the *Shiva Purana* or the *Shaiva Agama* texts, there is a continued reference to the shivalingam. There is plenty of evidence to demonstrate that people from pre-modern India associated the iconic form of the lingam to the male sexual organ. In his poem 'Garland of Games', the eleventh-century Kashmiri Sanskrit poet Kshemendra wrote, 'Having locked up the house on the pretext of venerating the lingam, Randy scratches her itch with a *lingam* of skin.' The same parallelism is even seen in the *Kamasutra*, as the translators write that they 'adroitly manage to escape the smell of obscenity,' by using what they presented as 'the Hindu terms for the sexual organs, yoni and lingam,' throughout their translation. Even though the use of lingam and yoni by Burton and Arbuthnot is problematic, because the terms do not represent the text, it was a deliberate ploy to avoid any kind of pornographic charges. Both Arbuthnot and Burton were well aware of the religious sanctity of the lingam and the yoni, as they said, 'There is in Hindustan an emblem of great sanctity, which is known as the Linga-Yoni.'

In fact, the deliberate use of the word 'lingam' in the *Kamasutra* even by Yashodhara, the thirteenth-century commentator of the text, was probably done to bring in the religious and the spiritual into a secular text. As Wendy Doniger writes, 'In fact, some Hindu traditions say that Shiva cannot be described or depicted so that an impersonal phallic stone is an appropriate symbol to express his divinity.'

Stella Kramrisch presents a deeply philosophical construct of Shiva in her book, *Presence of Shiva*. Shiva in his numerous manifestations is seen as a pillar of light, superior to the other two parts of the holy trinity of Brahma, the Creator, and Vishnu, the Preserver. Shiva appears in the form of a pillar of light shaped likes a penis, or lingam, through which both Brahma and Vishnu traverse trying to find a beginning and an end. Shiva asserts his supremacy by showing no beginning and no end to both Brahma and Vishnu, as the two are unable to end their journey. Shiva, also through this metaphor, expresses the timelessness of time, i.e. Mahakaal or the lord of time.

'In India, the lingam—the symbol of the creator-god Shiva—can be seen almost everywhere. Much less well-known are the fantasies involving mega-phalluses, which are most frequently depicted in wood carvings on the ceremonial wagons to carry images of the gods in procession, particularly in the southern part of the country.'

The lingam over the years has become the most forceful representation of Shiva, and every Shiva temple has the presiding deity as a shivalingam. The complete shivalingam is an erect penis, usually a simple, smoothly polished cylindrical or egg-shaped stone resting on a vagina-shaped base known as the gauri-patta or yoni, thus, showing the conjoining of the male and female principle. This is similar to the Greek concept of pleroma. The simple cylindrical shape of the lingam is the font of life and the entry into death. In a temple, the axis of the linga and the central peak of the temple roof are in a direct line—representing the lingam of light. The erect phallus is classified into three parts. The lowermost is square and concealed within the pedestal; it represents Brahma, the creator and the gravitational power and holds and shapes the universe. The second section is the octagonal section in the centre which symbolizes Vishnu, the main power which gives birth to matter. Lastly, the uppermost part is cylindrical and an emblem of Shiva, the powerful force of expansion. The base of the structure is none other than the yoni in which all matter realizes its individuality.

As Stella Kramrisch puts it, 'It is Shiva! This bit of polished rock is the tiny point (*bindu*) out of which springs divine manifestation. It is the ford (*tirtha*) over the treacherously turbulent streams of incarnation. It is the bridge connecting the ephemeral with the eternal, the conditioned with the absolute, and the hidden with the manifest.'

Most shivalingams in the temples of India, particularly in Andhra Pradesh, Karnataka and Tamil Nadu, and most of northern India, have stone lingas. Stone worship is a universal phenomenon going back to the prehistoric times. Many sanctified stones have been associated with spirits, fertility and as gateways to

The magnificient shivalingam found at Hampi.

other worlds—the Ka'aba in Mecca, the Greek Omphalos, the tomb of the sacred python in Delphi, the Rock of Ages, and the Semitic Beth-els, i.e. Bethlehem. The shivalinga, too, is an emblem of such archetypical sentiments.

While the lingam or Shiva as a concept or manifestation is not mentioned in the oldest book of knowledge of the Hindus, the Rig Veda clearly mentions Rudra, a manifestation of Shiva, as does the male organ, called 'kapruth' which could mean expanding or extending pleasure. According to some scholars, the Vedic god Indra is encouraged to strike down 'those whose god is the phallus' or those who take enjoyment in playing with the phallus. The word lingam does appear later, in the Upanishads, where it is also known as artha, as explained by Wendy Doniger.

The lingam: enfolded within the many myths of emergence

How can an icon of such immense power be free from the many myths which are part and parcel of Indic culture? Certain myths add to the grand narrative of Shiva and his lingam and explain the hold the lingam has over the popular imagination of philosophers, believers, artists and writers.

The story around the lingam stone found in the Samnihatya lake has been revered for long. It is believed that it was in this lake that Rudra, or another form of Shiva, had experienced his yogic trance. When his trance was over, in deep anger he tore out his phallus, which was then erected in the water. Since then the lingam has come to be known as sthanu. This further intertwines with the myths around the stone lingam. The same story is told in a different way in another text. In his retelling of the Shiva Purana, Ramesh Menon describes the falling of the lingam in the Deodhar forest, where angered by the Devas, Shiva threw his lingam and the fallen lingam burned everything in and around the forest. Stella Kramrisch, too, refers to the same myth in *The Presence of Shiva*: 'He willed his *linga* to fall. He severed it as an instrument of lust. The severance of the phallus was the purpose of his play. He played convincingly ... Though he aroused the women as the source of their desire, they were unable to see him as the killer of all desire.'

In the same myth, there is a projection of the union of the male and female—that of Shiva and Shakti, as seen in the Shiva Purana. When the shivalingam fell in the Deodhar forest it began to burn everything—from the earth to the heavens to the underworlds. The phallus wreaked raging havoc everywhere The Rishis and Devas rushed to Brahma for help.

Brahma said, 'Brahmanas, what a foolish thing you have done. As long as Shiva's *linga* ranges the worlds there will be no peace anywhere.'

The Rishis and the Devas cried out, 'How can we make the blazing thing still?' Brahma pondered a moment; then he said gravely. 'Worship Uma: only she can make Shiva's organ quiet.'

And hence, a jar of water from a holy tirtha was placed on an eight-petalled yantra, with sprouts of barley and durva grass, accompanied by the chanting of mantras from the Vedas. The wild lingam was drenched with the water from the sacred jar and the raging lingam was placated, though still throbbing, and materialized near the goddesses Yantra. The Devas and Rishis mounted the throbbing lingam on the pedestal of the yoni of Parvati. Along with chanting of Vedic hymns Shiva was worshipped anew with offerings of food, perfume, sandal, flowers, incense, music and prostrations. While Parvati assumed the form of the cosmic yoni, the shivalinga became still. 'Only the mountain daughter can bear my linga within her body. Now there shall be peace and fruitfulness; let the worlds prosper.'

This first phallus that fell out of Shiva's hand is known as Hataksema, Hatesa or *Siva-Siva*. Wherever Hatesa is worshipped there is joy in this life and moksha hereafter. Rita M. Gross in her essay, 'Hindu Female Deities as a Resource for the Contemporary Rediscovery of the Goddess', says: '*Shivalinga* is one of the androgynous forms of Shiva. In fact, the phallic *linga* is almost always accompanied by the yoni, the symbol of the Goddess's sexual organ, and as such is iconic, though not anthropomorphic, androgyny. In this form, the male is surrounded by the female, in the representation of sexual union. But the female may be androgynously within the male, as well; the Goddess is sometimes depicted emerging from inside the *Shivalinga*. This is an imitation of the epiphany of Siva himself in the myth of the *lingodbhava*.'

Kramrisch puts it rather succinctly, when she says: 'Between the explicitly phallic shape of the earliest *lingas* and the later, abstract pillar shape of the *linga* lay the symbolic saturation of this vertical sign with ontological meaning. Between the abstract pillar shape by itself and its setting in the yoni lay a return to the primary phallic meaning ... the *linga* in the *yoni* focuses on the sexual situation of coitus, introducing into it, however, the paradox of the *urdhvalinga* as a sign of *urdhvaretas*. The latter connotes the retention, ascent, and transformation of the seed within the body of the lord of yogis. The abstract, geometrical shape, however, of the *urdhvalinga*, the repository of the ontology of existence, placed on the yoni as its pedestal, rises out of the yoni, the womb; it does not enter it. The "linga in the yoni" emerges from the yoni; it does not penetrate it. This paradox in the coital proximity of the sexual symbols is consonant with and amplifies that of the *linga* itself.'

By extension, the lingam is also understood to be both the fountainhead of all desired and the holder of lust. 'They would touch but could not hold him who was

A shivaligam with the snake as a hood found at the Brihadishwan Shiva temple in Tamil Nadu.

free in frenzy and divine madness, the still core of the flame.' as Kramrisch puts it in *The Presence of Siva*. She further elucidates Shiva as Bhiksatana, the form Shiva adopted when he visited the Deodhar forest as the Supreme Beggar. As Bhiksatana, Shiva is represented as completely naked, yet he is adorned with unusual jewels, with a snake coiled around his hips as a bejewelled belt and the sky as his garment.

Kramrisch describes Shiva as, 'His *linga* is not raised. It conveys neither lust nor yogic control. Siva as Bhiksatana in the tradition of image-makers, appears in divine spontaneity, aloof from emotions that his maya/illusion proved in the rishis and their women.' The same myth is further explored by Wendy Doniger in her book, *Sexual Metaphors and Animal Symbols in Indian Mythology*, as well, 'When the pine (or cedar) forest myth appears in Tamil texts, however a notable change takes place, Siva enters the forest and women flock to him, but he is not castrated (which was the point of the myth in the Sanskrit texts); rather, when the sages attack him, he dances in such a way that their attacks are useless, and the sages and gods witness the dance of Nataraja there and worship him.' In this way, a purely sexual image of violence is translated into an image of a solitary, powerful, metaphorical dance.

In the Indian storytelling tradition, the lingam with its many metaphors and many allegories is a treasure trove of celebration in its many forms across literature, visual and performing arts. There is hardly any aspect of Indian thought which is not touched by the myth of the lingam or unaware of the simple strong cylindrical phallic shapes that are spread all over the countryside.

The Lingayats

Another way of understanding the lingam is through a sect of Shiva followers from Karnataka, known as Lingayats or the Veershivas, the founder of the sect being Basavanna. The word lingayat emerges from the Kaṇnada word 'lingavanta' or the one who wears an istalinga. The istalinga is an oval-shaped stone which symbolizes the parashiva or absolute reality. Made of light-grey slate, the ishtalinga is coated with a long-lasting paste of cow-dung ashes mixed with oil to make it durable and strong. The lingam is tied to the body of the male ever since he is born and it remains tied to the body till he dies. The establishers and followers of the sect wear the little shivalingam in a silver box, just like many devotees such as Christians wear a holy cross signifying the crucifixion Christ. This similarity could be traced to an influence from the nearby state of Kerala, that has a dominant number of Syrian Christian Catholics, who wear a cross around their necks. A description of this sect is seen in *Shiva: The Wild God of Power and Ecstasy*:

The devotees sing the following song:
'The rich will make temples for Shiva.
What shall I, a poor man, do?
My legs are pillars,
The body, the shrine,
The head, a cupola of gold.
Listen, O Lord of the Meeting Rivers,
Things standing shall fall
But the moving ever shall stay.'

The lingam, thus, is the metaphor for the individual religious and spiritual life. For a person, the formal entry into being a lingayat begins after the deeksha ceremony—rites of passage performed by the guru who initiates the person into the inner codes of the ligayatam traditions.

Markers of identity: the shivalinga and its classifications

Interestingly, Shiva is also worshipped in his anthropomorphic form. Despite that, the lingam occupies the centremost position in a Shiva temple—as seen in temples from the Pallava period, Shiva deities are placed a step lower than the lingam. There are many kinds of lingams but they are broadly divided into two categories—the movable chala-lingas or the immovable achala-lingas. Many sub-categories exist within these; an important one being the mukhalingas, which can have a number of faces of Shiva emerging from the central lingam. The chala-lingas are basically meant for personal worship and could be carried through the journeys and pilgrimages.

It is said that Ravana always carried a golden lingam with him for worship. As the lingam is always placed within a pedestrian, symbolizing the union of the penis and vulva, Ravana would place his idol of the golden lingam in sand, and would then perform prayers with incense and fragrant flowers. In the commentary to *Uttara-kanda*, it is said, '... that the golden *linga* was intended for constant worship. He worshipped it from the desire of sovereignty. For it is prescribed in the tantra that a golden *linga* should be worshipped when any one desires sovereignty.'

The chala-lingas are further divided into five different categories, according to the material they are made of. These are described below.

Mrinmaya, made of earth

For making these, white clay is collected from holy places, including river banks or hilltops, and a mixture is made with yogurt, milk, ghee, wheat flour, barley flour and sandal powder. The entire concoction is kept aside for a period of 20–30 days. Then according to the conditions given in the Agamas—ancient Hindu scriptures—the lingam is shaped in its form to the bring the downfall of the enemy.

The lingam at the Parashurameshvara temple.

Lohaja, made of metals

This lingam is made out of eight metals in their pure form, including brass, copper, bell-metal, gold, iron, lead, silver and tin.

Ratnaja, made of precious stones

Just like the one with metals, only seven precious stones can be used to make these lingams, such as bluestone, cat's-eye, corals, emeralds, pearls, quartz crystal and topaz.

Daruja, made of wood

Wood from trees such as arjuna, bilva, badara, chandana, devadaru, karnikara, khadira, madhuka, manduka, pippala, sala, sami and udumbara can be used to make this lingam. Alternatively, any other tree that oozes milky latex when its branch is broken can be used.

Sailaja, made of stone

These lingams are worn as an ornament by devotees belonging to the religious sect of Jangamas, Lingavantas or Lingayats, or Vira Saivas.

Kshanika, for one-time use

Often during religious ceremonies, lingams are made out of grass, flowers, flour, sand, raw rice, clay, sandal paste or rudraksha seeds. These need to be disposed off after the rituals are over.

Though the actual numbers of achala-lingas are contestable since various Agamas mention different figures, these could be divided into several categories as documented in the Suprabhedagama—Svayambhuva, Purva/Purana, Daivata, Ganapatya, Asura, Sura, Arsha, Rakshasa, Manusha and Bana. According to the influential *Kamikagama* there are six categories of these lingams: Svayambhuva, Daivika, Arshaka, Ganapatya, Manusha and Bana.

These achala-lingas are generally site-specific and found inside the sanctum sanctorum of the Shiva temples where they are the presiding deity.

Svayambhuva lingam

In India, the Svayambhuva lingam are found in sixty-eight places, according to *Jirnoddhara-dasakam* by Nigamajnanadeva of the Vyaghrapura clan, who was the son of Vamadevasivacharya. It is illustrated in the Kamakigama that these lingams have been present since time immemorial and that they ought to be protected by the king and his subjects. If these lingams were broken due to natural forces—fire, flood or in battle—they need not be restructured. But it is of importance to maintain the sanctity of the lingam by keeping it free from harmful pollutants. If a major portion of such a lingam needs to be fixed then it needs to be fixed with a layer of metals, copper and gold. In any major event, if the lingam is completely annihilated from the ground of its setting, then king and his kingdom would face dire consequences. In fact, a svayambhuva lingam is considered so sacred that it is above all the rules laid down in the Agamas for the other classes of lingams—it is no wonder that every village claims the 'svayambhuva' nature for lingams set up in its temple.

Daivika lingam

The Makutagama mentions Daivika lingams as the ones with an uneven surface. The lingam unequally rises and stoops low at certain sections and also carries craters that gives it the shape of a chisel and trident. Interestingly, these lingams look like a burning flame or even a pair of hands as if performing prayer. These lingams are without the Brahma or the parsvasutras.

Ganapa lingam and the Arsha lingam

The Ganapa lingams are made according to the set of codes laid out in the ganas, or the philosophers. They are in the shape of fruits including cucumber, citron, palm and wood-apple. Whereas, Arsha lingams look like a raw coconut with a lower section broader than the top section of the lingam. Like the Daivika lingams, these two also do not have the parsvasutras. It is mentioned in the Kiranagama that all three—Svayambhuva lingams, Ganapa lingams and Arsha lingams are without any rupa (shape) or mana (measurement) but are given these names due to the shapes.

Manusha lingam and Mukha lingam

With Manusha lingams, we have the largest number of achala or the sthavara lingams. It is made of human hands, as the name manusha suggests. These are made according to the conditions mentioned in the Agamas. These lingams could be made by taking the central shrine's doorway's height and the cubical length of the central shrine into consideration. The Mukha lingam can have more than one, two, three, four, five faces corresponding to the five facets of Shiva—Vamadeva, Tatpurusha, Aghora, Sadyojata and Isana.

The twelve pillars of light: the Jyotirlingas

'Jyoti' means radiance and linga means the mark of Shiva. The twelve jyotirlingas are the most important sites of Shiva's worship: Somanatha, Mallikarjuna, Mahakala, Parameswara, Kedara, Bhimashankara, Visvesa, Tryambaka, Vaidyanatha, Nagesa, Ramesa and Ghumesa. According to Hindu mythology, the world is divided into Devas, Asuras and the mortals, where Shiva rules with his sacred phalluses. The three temporal worlds of the Devas are pervaded by Shiva in the form of phalluses. However, the twelve jyotirlingas are spread in every region of the land. It is believed that at the site of the twelve jyotirlingas, Shiva showered his blessings with his reincarnation and his sacred lingam is a representation of his love towards the devotees. A prayer to these jyotirlingas, or even a mere sight of it, opens the path towards moksha—a devotee can get rid of his sins with daily prayers and offering to the jyotirlingas.

As stated above, the twelve jyotirlingas are the most sacred of religious pilgrimages for the Shaivaites. In their lifetime, Shaivaites would try to ideally visit all the twelve jyotirlingas. Each pilgrim is on his/her journey to experience the touch and feel of the sacred phallus.

Someshwar Somnath, Gujarat

Someshwar Somnath in western Gujarat is a special jyotirlinga. Shiva is known by many names at Somanth—Mrityunjaya, Kaalagnirudra, Amritesa, Anamaya, Kritivasa, Kaalbhairav and Bhairavanatha. The story behind the temple is an intriguing one. The Skanda Purana, in a chapter on Prabhasa Khanda, describes Somnath—Shiva in the previous aeons was referred to as Somnath. The shivalingam at Somnath is a bright and shining one. The story around the astounding brightness of the shivalingam is associated with the moon. It was said that Chandra, the moon was married to all twenty-seven daughters of Daksha Prajapati. However, the moon was partial to Rohini. As a result of which he was cursed by his father-in-law to disappear without a trace. Traumatized and unhappy, Chandra along with his wife Rohini worshipped the Sparsa Linga at Somnath. Pleased with Chandra's prayer, Shiva blessed him to shine as bright as a moon.

In 1024, the temple was ransacked by the Turko-Persian ruler Mahmud Ghazni. Several stories abound around the sack of Somnath. Al Biruni, an Iranian scholar, stated that the temple built of stone was constructed almost a hundred years before the sack of the temple by Ghazni. The temple was almost like a fortress surrounded by the sea on three sides since it needed to be heavily guarded because of the vast riches it owned. The surging tides came up to the temple as if the sea itself was worshipping the icon of the lingam.

Mallikarjuna temple, Andhra Pradesh

Known as the Kailash of the South, the Mallikarjuna temple is one of the greatest Shiva shrine of India. One of the stories in Shiva Purana, speaks of the intensity of Kartikeya's anger. He was angry because his younger brother Ganesh was

சிவ சிவ
சிவ சிவ சிவ சிவ சிவ சிவ சிவ சிவ சிவ சிவ சிவ சிவ சிவ சிவ

Many temples in India are dedicated to Shiva and house magnificent lingams. (Clockwise, left to right): The Meenakshi-Sundareshwara temple, the temple at Hampi in Karnataka, the Somnath temple, Thanjavur Brihadeeshwara temple, the Shiva temple at Bhojpur and the Parashurameshvara temple.

married before him. Enraged, he went away to the Kraunch mountains. None of the lords could appease him. Even his divine parents, Shiva and Parvati, were turned away by Kartikeya himself. Hurt, Shiva assumed the form of a jyotirlinga and started residing in this mountain taking on the name of Mallika–Arjuna, Mallika means Parvati and Arjuna is another name for Shiva. It is believed that just by seeing the tip of the mountain all sins are washed away and moksha is attained where the mortal becomes free of the cycle of life and death.

Mahakaleshwar, Madhya Pradesh

On the banks of the river Shipra and within the dense forest of Ujjain, lays this temple. The origins of the jyotirlinga here is based on the story of the five-year-old Shrikar who was captivated by the devotion of King Chandrasen of Ujjain towards Lord Shiva. Shrikar took a stone and started worshipping it as Shiva. In spite of a large number of people trying to stop him from worshipping the stone, Shrikar's devotion kept growing. Pleased by his reverence, Shiva took the form of a jyotirlinga and started living in the Mahakali forest. The Mahakaleshwar jyotirlinga is also one of the seven muktisthalls, a place of liberation.

Kedaranath, Uttarakhand

Holiest of the holy, the Kedarnath linga is at a height of about 12,000 feet on a mountain named Kedar.

According to a popular legend, Shiva was pleased by the austerities observed by Nara and Narayana, the two incarnations of Lord Vishnu. Because of their intense devotion Shiva took up permanent abode in the form of a jyotirlinga, which came to be known as the Kedarnath jyotirlinga. Due to its height this jyotirlinga can only be accessed for six months of the year. To visit this jyotirlinga there is a tradition that while embarking on a pilgrimage to the Kedarnath jyotirlinga, devotees first visit Yamunotri and then Gangotri, and finally bathe the Kedarnath lingam with the waters from the water collected from these two rivers. The popular belief is that the Kedarnath jyotirlinga is the wish-fulfilling lingam.

Bhimashankar, Maharashtra

The jyotirlinga at Bhimashankar is located on the banks of the river Bhima, in the Sahidrya region of Pune, Maharashtra. The story around this jyotirlinga is not clear; many intertwined stories abound. But many stories talk about Bhima, son of Kumbhkaran, the brother of Ravana. When Bhima learned that his father was killed by Vishnu, in his incarnation as Ram, he vowed to take his revenge on Vishnu. Bhima performed immense penance to please Brahma, who then gave Bhima immense power. The newly powerful Bhima started wreaking havoc on earth. The gods then requested Shiva to come to earth to bring peace. Shiva fought a great battle and killed the demon, and on request of the gods he made the forest his home and manifested himself as a jyotirlinga. It is said that the river Bhima was sweat which poured from Shiva's body after his battle with Bhima. It is a pilgrim's paradise and has rare species of flora and fauna.

Vishwanath, Varanasi

Kashi is one of the seven cities known as Mokshadayikas, a city that leads to salvation. Kashi, also known as Varanasi, has a temple for almost every Hindu god and goddess. It is in this city that Shiva also whispered the sacred chant of the Mahamrityunjaya mantra. It is here in the city that Shiva is known as the Lord of Universe Vishwanatha. The Avimukteshvara lingam is situated in the courtyard of Vishwanatha temple. It was destroyed by Qutb-ud-din Aibak in 1194 CE and rebuilt by Queen Ahalyabai Holkar of Indore in the eighteenth century. The shikar of the temple was gold-plated on the orders of Maharaja Ranjit Singh, which is why it is known as the golden temple of Varanasi.

Tryambakeshwar, Nashik

Situated in the eastern section of the Sahyadri, 30kms from Nashik and at the foothills of Brahmagiri, this temple is made out of black stone. The abode of the three-eyed god Shiva, the highlight of this jyotirlinga is that it has three faces coming out of the lingam, which represents the holy trinity. The lingam at Tryambakeshwar is covered by a crown made of emeralds, diamonds and many other precious stones.

The Ekambareswarar temple which has a Prithivi lingam.

Vaidyanath, Jharkhand

Located in the Deodar Santal Parganas region of Jharkhand, the Vaidyanath temple is one of the highly-revered jyotirlinga shrines. The story goes that Ravana, a great bhakt of Shiva, wanted Shiva to come to Lanka and make it invincible. Therefore, Ravana wanted to take the abode of Shiva, Mount Kailash, with him to Lanka. Shiva foiled his plan and Ravana went on to do more penance and requested Shiva again. Shiva, in turn, offered to give Ravana one of his pillars of light (one of the twelve jyotirlingas) on the condition that if the jyotirlinga is put on the ground it would get rooted to that spot till eternity. The legend goes that the god of water, Varun, entered Ravana's body and made him feel an intense need to relieve himself. Then Vishnu came to him in the guise of a young lad and promised to hold the lingam while Ravana went on with his business. Vishnu then placed the lingam on the ground, and it got rooted to the spot. Ravana was so distraught by this that he cut off one of his nine heads. It was Ravana's patron saint, who revived him and joined his head to the body like a vaidyanath or doctor. That is how this lingam came to be known as Vaidyanath.

Nageshwara, Gujarat

Once upon a time, an ardent devotee of Shiva, Supriya was captured by the demon, Daaruka. The demon imprisoned Supriya along with her friends and companions

The kubera lingam found at the Jambukesvara temple.

in his capital, Daarukavana. Supriya asked all her fellow prisoners to chant the mantra of Om Namah Shivaya. This angered Daaruka and he rushed to kill Supriya. Shiva then manifested himself in front of the demon and killed him. It was in this form that the Nageshwara jyotirlinga came into being. The temple of Nageshwara, also known as Nagnath Temple, is situated between Gomati Dwarka and the Bait Dwarka island on the coast of Saurashtra. This particular Nageshwara jyotirlinga is believed to protect all its devotees from all types of poisons.

Rameshwar, Rameswaram

On the way back to Ayodhya, Rama worshipped the lingam made out of the earth by Sita. Hanuman was given the task of bringing the image of Viswanathan from Varanasi, but since he got delayed, Ram chose to worship this form of Shiva at the auspicious hour. This is how this temple got the name of Rameshwar, and the city where it is located is called Rameswaram.

Grihshneshwar, Aurangabad

The story around the Grishneshwar temple is about a woman named Kusuma. Kusuma worshipped Shiva and would keep the shivalingam in a tank of water to purify it as a part of her prayers. This devotion to Shiva gained her respect among the people of her village. Her husband's other wife was very jealous of all the praise and ended up killing Kusuma's son. Such was the devotion of the woman that she didn't stop her worship but continued her prayers. According to another myth when Kusuma kept the lingam in the tank, her son came back to his life. Pleased with her, Shiva came to visit her and the village as Grihshneshwar jyotirlinga. Since then the temple has gained reverence among the devotees of the village and beyond.

Omkareshwara, Madhya Pradesh

Each and every jyotirlinga of Shiva has a particular myth attached to it. Normally it is a war between the good and the evil—the good is in the form of the Devas or gods, and the demons, who are also known as Danavas. On the island of Shivapuri, on the banks of the river Narmada, there was a war between the gods and the demons. As victory went to the demons, the gods fell at the feet of Shiva. The Devas prayed long and hard to Shiva, who then revealed himself as the Omkareshvara jyotirlinga and defeated the Danavas, bringing peace and harmony.

Lingam temples: Panchbhootas

Shivalingam temples are also known as Panchbhoota lingams—the five essential elements or the panchtattvas.

Traversing through the cornucopia of Indic knowledge, Shiva becomes the most appropriate metaphor for the five elements—earth, fire, ether, wind, water—an embodiment of the panchtattvas. This is most apparent in the five lingams or panchalingams that exist in four temples in Tamil Nadu and one in Andhra Pradesh. Each of these temples represent one of the five elements, the foundation of all creation. These five 'bhoota sthalams' are said to be the sites where the Lord Shiva took the form of one of the elements. Each sthalam is associated with a particular element and each of the five panchbhutalingams has a particular myth around it.

The Prithvi lingam, Earth

The Prithvi lingam, found in Tamil Nadu is known as the Ekambareswarar. The myth surrounding this temple centers on the story of Parvati, who was sitting deep in meditation under a tree. To see if she was a true devotee, Shiva set her alight. Wrapped in flames, Parvati beseeched her brother, Vishnu, to save her, and on hearing her prayers, Vishnu cooled Parvati down with the rays from the moon which crown Lord Shiva's head. Shiva also tested Parvati in other ways, like sending the river Ganga to disturb her, but she overcame this by fashioning a lingam out of sand and uniting with it when Lord Shiva appeared from within the lingam, thus taking her for his wife.

The Agni lingam, Fire

The Agni lingam's story is about power. A quarrel between Brahma and Vishnu ensued to decide who amongst the two was more powerful. This led to Shiva being asked to judge a competition to ascertain the answer. Shiva declared that the first to reach the crown or feet of the Agni lingam would be the winner. Lord Vishnu assumed the form of a swan and undertook a journey of many years to reach Shiva's crown, but he could only find a falling lotus flower. This flower was used to adorn Shiva's crown. Vishnu asked it how long it would take to reach the crown. The flower said it had fallen from Shiva's crown eons ago but still had not reached the bottom, so Vishnu used his powers to make the flower believe that it had seen Vishnu reach Shiva's crown. However, Shiva was not fooled, and in his anger, he assumed a furious, fiery form. On witnessing his terrible fury, Vishnu and Brahma begged Shiva to calm down, and this is when Shiva took on the form of the Agni lingam.

The Aagaya/ Akasha lingam, Ether

The Akasha lingam is where Shiva and Goddess Kali engaged in a cosmic dance contest and the lingam itself takes the form of the empty space that is meant to represent the vastness of consciousness.

The Vayu lingam, Wind

The presence of the vayu devta or wind deity that mysteriously sweeps through the temple is one of the reasons that makes this spot so hallowed. The story associated with the lingam tells of how it was worshipped by a snake, spider and elephant in their own ways. The spider spun a web around it, the elephant washed it with water from its trunk and the snake offered a jewel to it in reverence. These three devotees is what the temple is named after—Sri Kala Hasti.

The Appu lingam, Water

Parvati once attempted to interrupt Lord Shiva's penance, which Shiva was not happy about. He wanted her to atone for her act and sent her to earth to undertake penance in the Jambu forest. Here, the goddess fashioned out of the water of the Cauvery a lingam and began to worship it. This is the story of how the Appu lingam or water lingam, came to be.

What is common to and inherent in these tales are the twin pillars of resilience and regeneration that characterize the elements as well as form the spirit of the concept of shivalingam.

Shivalingam in living culture

'The foundation of the whole world is the phallus
Everything comes forth from the *lingam*.
He who would perfect his soul must worship the *lingam*'.
—*The Phallus in Art and Culture*

The worship of the phallus is still alive in India. As with most ancient cultures, the Sun God is a universal god or and within Indian culture, the Sun God or Surya becomes a part of the Hindu triad of Brahma, Vishnu and Mahesh. Brahma, the creator of the Universe is akin to the rising sun, Vishnu the preserver is the mid-day sun and Shiva the destroyer is the god of the setting sun. The phallus or the lingam of Shiva is the symbol of the creative power of Shiva—as Shiva is credited with the power of being able to hold back his seed and therefore is an erect phallus. The lingam becomes the potential creator. The Shiva Purana states, '... it is not the phallus itself that is worshipped, but what the phallus represents, the Creator, the Cosmic Person. The Phallus is the emblem the sign and symbol of the God Shiva.'

Shiva, because of his ability to withhold his semen is thus the mahayogi and the mahabhogi, the erotic ascetic. As the yogi, he is the god of Yoga, and through yogic practice he achieves control over all carnal desires—one of the primary aims of yoga. Through yoga it is believed that the procreative seed travels from the lowest chakra to the highest chakra in the human spine and transforms sexual energy into mental energy. This is the highest form of yogic discipline. The Naga sadhus, who are still present in India, are a living statement of this aspect of yogic control. The Naga sadhus walk around naked, some of them stretch their penis to such an extent that they can be wound around a stick and are seen at the sacred Kumbh melas, the Maha Kumbh, which occurs every twelve years, and the Ardh Kumbh which occurs every six years. In the Purusha Sukta it is written: 'worshipping the *lingam* does not mean honouring a physical organ, but simply the recognition of an eternal and divine form which manifests itself in the cosmos. The human organ is only an image of this divine emblem, the original archetype, the *lingam*.'

A Naga sadhu.

Within indigenous societies of India, Shiva is part of their environment as an agriculturalist, as Pasupati, the god of animals. Shiva is known as Mahadeo to the farmer, Bardeo or Lingopen to the Gonds, a tribal community in central India and Baba Deo to the largest of group of tribals, the Bhil community of Rajasthan, Madhya Pradesh, Andhra Pradesh and Gujarat and parts of Sindh in Pakistan. The Kol worship a mountain god known as Morang Buru or Bar Pahad, as the form of the mountain are considered symbols of strength, vigour and vitality. The fact that they sometimes resemble the form of the human phallus associates mountains with svayambhulingams, or self-wrought phalluses. In fact many deities of the Toda community are hill deities shaped like phalluses.

A wall painting with Shiva found at Haveli Kedia, Fatehpur.

The sacred, the profane and the popular

Be it the illustrations of the Ramayana, Mahabharata, the Puranas, or in the indigenous narratives of the tribal cultures of India, Shiva is everywhere. In the popular traditions, be it scroll-paintings of Bengal or Rajasthan, Kalamkari of Andhra Pradesh, the vibrant tradition of Kerala murals or in the tradition of classical dance, the shivalingam is a popular icon.

The shivalingam is a recurring motif in the sacred, profane and popular. From the inner sanctum of temples to cinema posters, myriad examples of the shivalingam have been painted by artists. From the Rajasthani miniature paintings or handheld paintings of the Raga Ragini to the delicate Pahari miniatures, the worship of the shivalingam is beautifully interpreted and painted. The shivalingam becomes the object of devotion by the nayika or heroine. Often, the nayika is shown either by herself or surrounded by her attendants worshipping the lingam as a metaphor for Shiva. She could be seeking either a husband of her choice or for the longevity of her husband since Shiva is the ideal mate and the complete benefactor of conjugal bliss. Often the ragini is also represented as a devotee of Shiva, and thus as the ragini Bhairavi is shown worshipping the lingam. The variety of calendar art, which is part of many Indian households has images of Shiva and Parvati with a shivalingam either in the foreground or the background. These large calendars serve as icons of worship in homes and in commercial small kiosks where the owners burn incense and make offerings of flowers. The calendar with the shivalingam becomes the altar of worship thus bringing the linga into the private and public spaces.

What makes Shiva, the dangerously feared god of death, the destroyer of life, keeper of time, the cool god of the contemporary times? The virile god with an erect penis, he had robust sex with his wife Parvati and even the male lord Vishnu in the form of Mohini, the androgynous form of Shiva–Shakti. Thus, the lingam of Shiva literally is hoisted aloft. The myth of Shiva and his phallus is still alive and kicking in the contemporary times of hybridity, cosmopolitanism and internationalism.

Wendy Doniger writes about the fascination of the youth and millennials towards their very own interpretations of Shiva's sexuality and sexual libido (the Shaivaite phallus being a popular motif): 'Shiva has always been hot, but I must confess that I was surprised—pleasantly surprised—to learn that he is now also cool, at least among young people in India. And not just cool but chic, fashionable. Young people of both sexes are wearing *rudrakshas* as accessories, dancing to Shiva music, indulging in Shiva tattoos, reading Shiva fiction. Some of them, it is rumoured, are even consuming bhang, as Shiva does. Where will all this end? Will the bright young things in their *rudrakshas* also start wearing freshly bloody elephant skins, and using live snakes to hold up their jeans? Will they stop combing their hair, or wear dreadlocks?'

Can we graphically imagine the world as a phallic shape/symbol? In Hindu sacred geography, the universe or brahmanda is the world as visualized, often conceived as a phallic space by traditional Indian artists and poets. What is interesting to note is that the shivlingam/phallus traverses with easy mobility from the innermost sacred space of the sanctum sanctorum to being tattooed on the bodies of devotees. He is the chillum-holding, pot-smoking god that appeals to the young, dope-smoking and intoxicated youth of today. Shiva becomes an icon for trance music lovers and is regularly painted on t-shirts by fashionistas and 'invoked' by the chants of '*bum bum bhole*,' '*dum maro dum*.' In a way, Shiva embodies a kind of sinister eroticism.

From architecture to automobiles, the phallic Qutab Minar in New Delhi to the gearbox in the cars, the form of the phallus is omnipresent. Primitive phallic stones to hot dogs, the association could be a happy coincidence for phallic worshippers around the world, or it could be deeply symbolic. As envisaged in the Indian cultural tradition, it is the imagined eye which sees that the phallus is everywhere. The phallus has been celebrated for centuries as a tool of fertility,

Shiva has transcended into popular culture with young people attaching him to music, drug-fuelled trances, clothing, and popular literature.

power and magic, and in contemporary times it is a cultural marker or identity, sexuality, power and masculinity. The shape, the metaphor and sanctity of the phallus is an all-encompassing representation which is undoubtedly celebrated in all its glory through high art and popular culture.

References and Bibliography

Introduction

Dworkin, J. Fateman and A. Scholder, *Last Days at Hot Slit: The Radical Feminism of Andrea Dworkin* (Cambridge: MIT Press, 2019), 108

Jacques Derrida, *Writing and Difference* (Chicago: The University of Chicago Press, 1978)

The phallus across eastern Asia

Marc Domsky, *Phallus Through Bhutan – Journey of the Magic Thunderbolt*, (Wyoming: Magic Thunderbolt, 2015)

C. Bendick, "Phallusdarstellungen in Bhutan", *Urologe*, 49, (2010), 1535–1542

M. Brauen, *Irgendwo in Bhutan*, (Frauenfeld: Waldgut, 1994)

Eibl-Eibesfeldt I., *Similarities and Differences between Cultures in expressive Movements*, in: R.A. Hinde: *Non-verbal Communications*, (Cambridge: Cambridge University press, 1979)

G. Chesi, "Palat Khik, der Phallus der Wunder wirken kan", in A4, *Magazin für Aussereuropaïscher Kunst und Kultur*, (January, 2007), 52–55.

C. Hemmet, "le Pays au million d'Amulettes", *La Thaïlande*, La revue du Musée de l'Homme, Tome 26, fascicule 1-2, (Paris: 1989), 49–64

Jean-Pierre Abel-Rémusat: *Description du royaume de Cambodge par un voyageur chinois qui a visité cette contrée à la fin du XIII siècle, précédée d'une notice chronologique sur ce même pays*, extraite des annales de la Chine, Imprimerie de J. Smith, 1819

Zhou Daguan, *The Customs of Cambodia*, (Cambodia: The Siam Society, 1992).

Ann R. Kinney, Marijke J. Klokke and Lydia Kieven, *Worshipping Siva and Buddha: The Temple Art of East Java*, (Honolulu: University of Hawaii Press, 2003).

M. Moens, *De iconografie van Shiva in het Hindoeïsme – een vergelijkende psychologische studie*, Licentiaatsthesis, (Leuven: 1996).

Theodore Bowie, et all, *Studies in Erotic Art*, (New York-London: Basic Books Inc., 1970).

W.G Aston, *Nihongi, Chronicles of Japan from the Earliest Times to A.D.697*, (London: The Japan Society, 1896).

Genchi Kato, *A study of the development of religious ideas among the Japanese people as illustrated by Japanese phallicism*, (Tokyo: Asiatic Society of Japan, 1924).

Stephen Turnbull, *Japan's Sexual Gods: Shrines, Roles and Rituals of Procreation and Protection*, volume 49, (Brill Academic Pub, 2015), 95.

Ibidem p.118.

P. Rawson, *Primitive Erotic Art*, (New York: G.P. Putnam's Sons, 1973).

M. Moes and E. Mitamura, "Mitamura Engyo zenshū", volume 21, (Jônuri to sekkyô, Ningyô sibai to Nô, Chūô Kôronsha, 1977).

M. Hayakawa, translated by C. Andrew Gerstle, *Shunga*: Ten Questions and Answers, Nichibunken Monograph Series n°14, (Kyoto: International Research Centre for Japanese Studies, 2013)

Andrew Markus, *Prostitutes and Prosperity in the Works of Terakado Seiken, Sexuality and Edo Culture* 1750–1850, (Bloomington: Indiana University, 1966).

Ibidem

Fujiwara no Akihira, Kawaguschi Hisao ed., *Shin sarugaku ki*, (Record of New Monkey Music), (Tokyo: Heibonska, 1983).

Johan J. Mattelaer, *From Ornamentation to Mutilation: Genital Decorations and Cultural Operations in the Male*, (Arnhem: The Historical Committee of the European Association of Urology, 2004).

The phallus in psychoanalysis: definition, fantasies and the role of geography

J. Benjamin, "Samness and Difference: Towards an Overinclusive Model of Gender Development", (Psychoanalytic Inquiry, 1995), 15(1): 125–142

D. Birksted-Breen, "Phallus, Penis And Mental Space", (Int. J. Psycho-Anal, 1996), 77: 649–657.

D. Birksted-Breen, "Feminine Sexuality. Jacques Lacan and the École Freudienne", (Int. J. Psycho-Anal., 1983), 64: 490–493.

R.J. Benton, "The Aufhebung of the Phallus", (Psychoanal. Contemp. Thought, 1995), 18(1): 53–74,

C. Bonomi, "Narcissism as mastered visibility: The evil eye and the attack of the disembodied gaze", (Int. Forum Psychoanal, 2010), 19(2):110-119

J. Butler, "Melancholy Gender—Refused Identification", (Psychoanal. Dial., 1995), 5(2):165–180

J. Chasseguet-Smirgel, "Freud and Female Sexuality—The Consideration of Some Blind Spots in the Exploration of the 'Dark Continent'". (Int. J. Psycho-Anal., 1976), 57:275–286

N. Chodorow, *The reproduction of mothering: Psychoanalysis and the sociology of gender*, (Berkeley, CA: University of California Press, 1978).

K. Corbett, M. Dimen, V. Goldner, and A. Harris, Talking Sex, Talking Gender—A Roundtable (Stud. Gend. Sex, 2014), 15(4):295–317.

W. Doniger, D. Sharma ed, "When a Lingam is Not Just a Good Cigar" in *Psychoanalysis, Culture and Religion: Essays in honour of Sudhir Kakar*, (Oxford University Press, 2014).

T. Ewens, "Female Sexuality and the Role of the Phallus", (Psychoanal. Rev., 1976–77), 63(4):615–637.

S. Freud, New Introductory Lectures on Psychoanalysis, Standard Edition, Vol. 22, (London: Hogarth Press, 1964), pp. (a) 114; (b) 115; (c) 116; (d) 131

G. Herdt and R. Stoller, *Intimate Communications: erotics and the study of culture*, (New York: Columbia University Presss, 1990).

G. Herdt, *The Guardians of the Flute. Idioms of Masculinity*, (USA: University of Chicago Press, 1982)

S. Kakar, *The Inner World: A Psychoanalytic Study of Childhood and Society in India*, (Delhi: Oxford India Perennials, 2012).

Kakar, S. (1989). The Maternal-Feminine in Indian Psychoanalysis. Int. Rev. Psycho-Anal., 16:355-362

S. Kakar, *The Analyst and the Mystic IN Indian Identity*, (New Delhi: Penguin Books, 1996), 172

S. Kakar, *Last Claims: psychoanalysis and the ageing sexuality of men and women*, manuscript submited for publication, (2019).

R.J. Stoller and G.H. Herdt, "The Development of Masculinity: A Cross-Cultural Contribution", (J. Amer. Psychoanal. Assn., 1996), 30:29–59

1. Vanggaard Thorkil, *Phallos: A Symbol and Its History In The Male World*, (London: Jonathan Cape, 1969).
D. Birksted-Breen, "Phallus, Penis And Mental Space", (Int. J. Psycho-Anal., 1996), 77:649–657.

2. Loc.cit

3. Vanggaard Thorkil, Phallos: A Symbol and Its History In The Male World, (London: Jonathan Cape, 1969).

4. R.J. Benton, "The Aufhebung of the Phallus", (Psychoanal. Contemp. Thought, 1995), 18(1):53–74.

5. Op.cit, Birkstead-Breen, (1996).

6. S. Kakar, *The Inner World: A Psychoanalytic Study of Childhood and Society in India*, (New Delhi: Oxford India Perennials, 2012), 187.

7. W. Doniger, D. Sharma ed, "When a Lingam is Not Just a Good Cigar" in *Psychoanalysis, Culture and Religion: Essays in honour of Sudhir Kakar*, (Oxford University Press, 2014).

8. K. Corbett, M. Dimen, V. Goldner and A. Harris, Talking Sex, Talking Gender—A Roundtable, (Stud. Gend. Sex., 2014), 15(4):295–317

9. S. Kakar, "The Maternal-Feminine in Indian Psychoanalysis", (Int. Rev. Psycho-Anal., 1989), 16:355–362

10. D. Birksted-Breen, "Phallus, Penis And Mental Space", (Int. J. Psycho-Anal., 1996), 77:649–657

11. D. Birksted-Breen, *Feminine Sexuality. Jacques Lacan and the École Freudienne*, (Int. J. Psycho-Anal., 1983), 64:490–493.

12. Ibid.

13. S. Kakar, *Last Claims: psychoanalysis and the ageing sexuality of men and women*, Manuscript submited for publication (2019).

14. S. Kakar, The Inner World: A Psychoanalytic Study of Childhood and Society in India <italics>, (New Delhi: Oxford India Perennials, 2012), 187

15. Op.cit Kakar. p.188

16. Loc.cit

17. C. Bonomi, "Narcissism as mastered visibility: The evil eye and the attack of the disembodied gaze", (Int. Forum Psychoanal., 2010), 19(2):110–119.

18. Ibid.

19. Ibid.

20. S. Kakar, *The Inner World: A Psychoanalytic Study of Childhood and Society in India*, (New Delhi: Oxford India Perennials, 2012).

21. Ibid.

22. Op.cit. Ewens

23. S. Freud, *New Introductory Lectures on Psychoanalysi*, (London: Hogarth Press, 1964), pp. (a) 114; (b) 115; (c) 116; (d) 131.

24. D. Birksted-Breen, Juliet Mitchell and Jacqueline Rose, eds., *Feminine Sexuality: Jacques Lacan and the École Freudienne*, (London: Macmillan, 1982), 187.

25. S. Kakar, S, *Last Claims: psychoanalysis and the ageing sexuality of men and women*, manuscript submited for publication, (2019).

26. Ibid, 132

27. N.Chodorow, *The reproduction of mothering: Psychoanalysis and the sociology of gender*, (Berkely, CA: University of California Press, 1978).

28. J. Butler, "Melancholy Gender—Refused Identification", (Psychoanal. Dial., 1995), 5(2):165–180.

29. Op.cit Benjamin

30. R.J. Stoller and G.H. Herdt, *The Development of Masculinity: A Cross-Cultural Contribution*, (J. Amer. Psychoanal. Assn., 1982), 30:29–59.

31. Ibid.

32. G. Herdt and R. Stoller, *Intimate Communications: erotics and the study of culture*, (New York: Columbia University Presss, 1990), 66

33. G. Herdt, *The Guardians of the Flute: Idioms of Masculinity*, (USA: University of Chicago Press, 1982).

34. Ibid.

35. Ibid.

36. Vanggaard Thorkil, *Phallos: A Symbol and Its History In The Male World*, (London: Jonathan Cape,1969), 39

37. Ibid., 25

38. Loc.cit.

39. Loc.cit.

40. Ibid. Thorkil, 34

41. Ibid. Thorkil, 42.

42. Op.cit Thorkil, 43
43. S. Kakar, *The Analyst and the Mystic IN Indian Identity*, (New Delhi: Penguin Books,1996), 172
44. Ibid.
45. Loc.cit, 176
46. R.J. Benton, "The Aufhebung of the Phallus", (Psychoanal. Contemp. Thought, 1995), 18(1):53–74
47. Ibid.
48. Op.cit Stoller
49. John Keats, quoted in S. Kakar, Entre-Vista Interview, (2019)
50. A. Narayanan, ed, *The Parrots of Desire: 3000 years of Indian erotica*, (New Delhi: Aleph Books, 2017)
51. S. Kakar, *Indian Identity*, (New Delhi: Penguin Books,1996), 132
52. E. Easwaran, *The Upanishad s*(Mumbai: Jaico Books,2010), 8
53. Ibid.
54. Ibid.

The phallus in Europe

George Scott, *Phallic Worship–A History of Sex & Sexual Rites*, (London: Luxor Press, 1966)
C. Eva Keuls, *The Reign of the Phallus–Sexual Politics in Ancient Athens*, (California: University of California Press, 1985)
R.P. Knight, *An Account of the Remains of the Worship of Priapus lately existing at Isernia, in the Kingdom of Naples in two Letters*, Printed by T. Spilsburg, Snowhill, 1786
Richard Payne Knight, *Le Culte de Priape et les rapports avec la Théologie mystique des Anciens*, (Paris: Eric Losfeld, 1989)
P.H. Brenot, *Male Impotence–A Historical Perspective*, (L'Esprit du Temps, 1994)
G. Ryley Scott, *Phallic Worship. A History of Sex & Sexual Rites*, (London: Senate, 1996)
Jacques Dupuis, *Au Nom du Père*, (Monaco/Paris: Le Rocher, 1987)
Özgen Acar, *Anatolia: The Land of the Father God. In: The History of Male and Female Sexuality and Fertility in Asia Minor*, M. Kendirci, A. Kadioglu, C.Miroglu, eds, (Istanbul: Turkish Society of Andrology, 2003), 89
B. Tascioglu, *Gods and Goddesses*, (Ankara: Anadolu Medeniyetleri Müzesi, 1992), 40
M. David Friedman, *A Mind of its Own: A Cultural History of the Penis*, (London: Robert Hale, 2002)
ibidem
K. Sethe, *Die Altägyptischen Pyramiden Texte*, 4th edition, (Leipzig, 1908–1922)
Vernus Pascal, *Le Papyrus de Turin et la Pornographie dans l'Egypte ancienne*, in: Andreu-Lanoë G.(ed) *L'Art de Contour, le dessin dans l'Egypte ancienne*, p.108-117, Paris, 2013
M. David Friedman, *A Mind of Its Own*, (London: Robert Halle, 2002).
C. Eva Keuls, *The Reign of the Phallus: Sexual Politics in Ancient Athens*, (New York: Harper & Row, 2002), 16
J. Davenport, *Aphrodisiacs and love stimulants*, (London: Luxor press, 1965)
A. Danielou, *Le Phallus*, (Puiseaux: Paedès, 1993)
Torkill Vanggaard, *Phallos*, (Kobenhavn: Gyldendal Nordisk Forlag, 1969)
Ibidem
Wijnand Van der Sanden and Torsten Capelle, *Götter Götzen Holzmenschen*, (Oldenburg: Isensee Verlag, 2002)
G. Anderson G. and L.B. Jörpeland, e.a., *Att föora gudarnas talan*, (Stockholm: Riksantikvarieämbtetet, 2004)
Richard Payne Knight, *Le Culte de Priape et les rapports avec la Théologie mystique des Anciens*, (Paris : Eric Losfeld, 1989), 114
Quoted by G. Rattray Taylor, in: *Sex in History*, (Harper & Row, 1953), 228

Colin Wilson, foreword in *The Roots of Witchcraft*, by Harrison Michael, (London: Frederich Muller, 1973), 18

H.J.E van Beuningen and A.M. Koldeweij, *Heilig en Profaan: 1000 laatmiddeleeuwse insignes*, (Nederland: Rotterdam Papers VIII. Cothen, 1993)

A.M. Koldeweij, *The Fascinating Faces of Flanders*, (Antwerp: Hessenhuis, 1998), 164–165

F. Bouchin, *2000 Years of Fashion*, (New York: Henry N.Abrams Inc., 1987), 240

Vicary G.W., *Visual Art as Social Data: the Renaissance*, Cultural Anthropology, 4, p.3, 1989

Jeffrey Russell, *Witchcraft in the Middle Ages*, (Cornell University Press, 1972), 4–10

Bengt Ankarloo And Stuart Clark, *Witchcraft and Magic in Europe: Biblical and Pagan Societies*, (University of Philadelphia Press, 2001)

Sarah Denning, *Mythology of Sex*, (New York: Macmillan, 1996)

Renilde Vervoort, *De zaak van de gestolen fallussen*, (Millenium Tijdschrift voor middeleeuwse studies, 22, 1, 2008), 3–23

Johan J. Mattelaer, *Witches and Sex, Cats and Stolen Phalluses in Medieval and Renaissance Europe*, (Arnhem: De Historia Urologiae Europaeae, vol 25, 2018), 81–98

Exempla in classical, medieval and Renaissance literature, consists of lives of famous figures, and using these (by emphasizing good or bad character traits) to make a moral point.

Georg Ferzoco, *The Massa Marittima Mural*, (Florence: Toscana Studies, 2004)

Johan J. Mattelaer, *The Phallus Tree: A Medieval and Renaissance Phenomenon*, (Journal of Sexual Medicine 7:2, 846-51, 2010)

J. Sjocher, *Eros sublime*, in De Facto - Magazine de l'Histoire de l'Art et de l'Archéologie, 4, p.5, 1993

D'Hooghe Alain, *Le sexe in photographiable*, (De facto - Magazine de l'Histoire de l'Art et d'Archéologie, 4, 1993), 32

Paolo Leonardi, *François Schuiten: J'éprouve du plaisir à dessiner des corps de femmes*, (De Facto - Magazine d'Histoire et d'Archéologie, 4, 1993), 46

Joop De Boer and Jaap van Linden, *Nathalie : la petite hôtesse*, (Paris: Editions Dessis, 1984)

Jim Chabane, *L'érection*, (France: Grand Angle, Bamboo Edition, 2016)

Power and Ecstasy: the cult of the lingam

B. Bhattacharya, *Saivism and the Phallic World*, (New Delhi: Munshiram Manoharlal Publishers Pvt. Ltd, 1993)

A. Danielou, *Gods of Love and Ecstasy: The Traditions of Shiva and Dionysus*, (Vermont: Rochester, Bear & Co, 1992)

Rita M. Gross, *"Hindu Female Deities as a Resource for the Contemporary Rediscovery of the Goddess"*, (Journal of the American Academy of Religion, vol. 46, no. 3, 1978, JSTOR), (www.jstor.org/stable/1463798. Accessed 27 Jan. 2020), 269–291

Sudhir Kakar, "Reflections on Psychoanalysis, Indian Culture and Mysticism", (*Journal of Indian Philosophy* 10 (3):289-297, 1982)

Kshemendra, *The Courtesan's Keeper*, Tr. Samaya Matrika, A.N.D. Haksar, (New Delhi: Penguin India, 2014)

Stella Kramrisch, *The Presence of Shiva*, (New Delhi: Motilal Banarsidass, 1988)

Raksha Kumar, "India Is Weaponizing its Spiritual Tourists", (https://foreignpolicy.com/2017/08/09/india-is-weaponizing-its-spiritual-tourists/), accessed on January 20, 2020.

Mat McDermott, "Why Are Journalists So Concerned About Penises in Hinduism?" (https://www.hafsite.org/blog/why-are-journalists-so-concerned-about-penises-in-hinduism/), accessed on January 23, 2020.

Johan J. Mattelaer, *Forbidden Fruit: Sex Eroticism Art*, (Davisfonds Uitgeverij, 2016).

Johan J. Mattelaer, *The Phallus in Art and Culture*, (Historical Committee of the European Association of Urology, 2000)

Madhavi Menon, *A History of Desire in India*, (New Delhi: Speaking Tiger, 2018)

Ramesh Menon, *The Shiva Purana Retold*, (New Delhi: Rupa Publications, 2010)

Wendy Doniger, *God's Body, or, The Lingam Made Flesh: Conflicts over the Representation of the Sexual Body of the Hindu God Shiva*, (New York: The John Hopkins University Press, 2011)

Wendy Doniger, *Sexual Metaphors and Animal Symbols in Indian Mythology*, (Chicago: University of Chicago Press, 1980)

Wendy Doniger, *On Hinduism*, (New York: Oxford University Press, 2014)

Wendy Doniger, "Shiva, The God of Cool Things" (https://www.pressreader.com/india/india-today/20130422/281904475653234), (accessed on 23 January, 2020).

Wendy Doniger and Sudhir Kakar, eds., Kamasutra, (New Delhi: Oxford University Press, 2009)

Alka Pande, *Indian Erotica*, (New Delhi: Roli Books, 2001)

Alka Pande, *Ardhanarishvara: The Androgyne Probing the Gender Within*, (New Delhi: Rupa and Co., 2004)

Alka Pande, *Masterpiece of Indian Art*, (New Delhi: Lustre Press, Roli Books, 2004)

Alka Pande, Leela – *An Erotic Play of Verse and Art*, (New Delhi: HarperCollins, 2009)

Alka Pande, *Shringara: The Many Faces of Indian Beauty*, (New Delhi: Rupa and Co., 2011)

Alka Pande, *Bodysutra: Tracing the human form through art and imagination*, (New Delhi: Rupa and Co., 2019)

Alka Pande, *Panchtattvas: The Road Ahead*, (New Delhi: Niyogi Books, 2017)

Purusha Suktam, (http://www.sathyasaiottawa.org/pdf/Vedam/Purusha_Suktam.pdf), (accessed on January 24, 2020).

T.A. Gopinath Rao, *Elements of Hindu Iconography: second edition*, (New Delhi: Motilal Banarsidass Publishers, 1997)

Eric Robertson, *The Penetrated Male: Phallic Feedback, the Male Hole, and Imposture*, (http://sites.uci.edu), 2012

J.L. Shastri, *The Shiva Purana*, (New Delhi: Motilal Banrasidas Publishers, 1930)

Wolf-Dieter Storl, *Shiva: The Wild God of Power and Ecstasy*, (New York: Simon and Schuster, 2002)

Romila Thapar, *The Many Voices of a History*, (New Delhi: Penguin Viking, 2004)

Vatsyayana, *Kama Sutra of Vatsyayana*, translated by Sir Richard Burton & F. F. Arbuthnot, (New Delhi: Penguin Books India, 2009)

Sameer Yasir and Ellen Barry, "Attack on Hindu Pilgrims' Bus in Kashmir Leaves 7 Dead", (https://www.nytimes.com/2017/07/10/world/asia/hindu-pilgrims-kashmir-shooting.html), (accessed on January 22, 2020).

Image credits

All images, unless stated otherwise, are from the private collections of Johan J. Mattelaer and Philip Van Kerrebroeck. The listed images follow in the order they appear in the book.

Contents

Anil Relia Collection, Ahmedabad, India

Introduction

Atid Kiattisaksiri/LightRocket via Getty Images, (https://www.gettyimages.in/detail/news-photo/naga-sadhu-shows-the-release-of-passion-by-lifting-large-news-photo/474926207)

Beroze and Michael Sabatier Collection, La Rochelle, France

Anil Relia Collection, Ahmedabad, India

The phallus across eastern Asia

Anthony Plowright

Anthony Plowright

National Museum of Indonesia, Jakarta. By courtesy of Prof. Dr. Rainy Umbas

The phallus in psychoanalysis: definitions, fantasies and the role of geography

Narasimha Prakash—Own work, CC BY-SA 3.0, (https://commons.wikimedia.org/w/index.php?curid=21162895)

Guildhall Library & Art Gallery/Heritage Images/Getty Images, (https://www.gettyimages.in/detail/news-photo/the-pyrrhic-dance-1869-dorian-warriors-performing-the-dance-news-photo/464494543)

The phallus in Europe

The British Museum

Mark Thorn, Taboo no more, Shalposky Publishers, New York, 1990

Javier Angulo

Muamer Kendirci

Allard Person Museum Amsterdam

J.F. Champollion, Panthéon Egyptien, Paris, 1923

Museum of Athens

Haddad Family Collection / Archeological Museum Naples / Archeological Museum Ephese

Archeological Museum Tarquina Viterbo

Carved phalluses in Pompeii, Sabratha, Clunia

Statens Historiska Museum Stockholm

Phallusses on Romanesque churches: Artaiz Navarra, St. Christophers Church, Courpiac, St. Petrus Church, Champagnolles, Giverzac, Charentes Maritimes, Saint- Palais Gironde, St. Stephens's Cathedral Vienna

Museum van Beuningen Rotterdam

(Left): Kunsthistorisches Museum, Hofjagd- und Rüstkammer Vienna, (right): The Metropolitan Museum of Art New York

(Clockwise, left to right) Kunsthistorisches Museum Vienna, Museo del Prado Madrid, Kunsthistorisches Museum Vienna, Galeria degli Uffizi Florence, Pinacotera di Brera Milan, Palazzo Pitti Florence

Vatican Museum, Ashmolean Museum Oxford, Stichting Cultureel Erfgoed Zeeland

The British Museum London

Rijksmuseum Amsterdam

Museum Voorlinden Wassenaar

(Center) Philadelphia Museum of Art

(Right) Museum of Contemporary Art Chicago

Power and ecstasy: the cult of the lingam

The Metropolitan Museum of Arts, New York

Ms Sarah Welch–Own work, CC BY-SA 4.0, (https://commons.wikimedia.org/w/index.php?curid=62840991)

(Top) Ms Sarah Welch–Own work, CC BY-SA 4.0, (https://commons.wikimedia.org/w/index.php?curid=62896896) and (https://commons.wikimedia.org/w/index.php?curid=62896908)

KennyOMG–Own work, CC BY-SA 4.0, (https://commons.wikimedia.org/w/index.php?curid=59878507)

Rijksmuseum, The Netherlands,

(https://useum.org/artwork/Vrouwen-voor-een-linga-altaar-Bhairavi-ragini-Unknown-Artist-1770)

Arun Varadarajan–Own work, CC BY-SA 3.0, (https://commons.wikimedia.org/w/index.php?curid=21192415)

Richard Mortel from Riyadh, Saudi Arabia– (74), CC BY 2.0, (https://commons.wikimedia.org/w/index.php?curid=64004411)

Bernard Gagnon–Own work, CC BY-SA 3.0,

(https://commons.wikimedia.org/w/index.php?curid=35565745)

(clockwise, left to right)

KennyOMG–Own work, CC BY-SA 4.0, (https://commons.wikimedia.org/w/index.php?curid=59878507)

Rajeshodayanchal–Own work, CC BY-SA 4.0, (https://commons.wikimedia.org/w/index.php?curid=68338925)

B. SurajPatro1997–Own work, CC BY-SA 4.0, (https://commons.wikimedia.org/w/index.php?curid=81648914)

Arian Zwegers–Thanjavur, Brihadishwara Temple, CC BY 2.0, (https://commons.wikimedia.org/w/index.php?curid=24487518)

Bernard Gagnon– Own work, CC BY-SA 3.0, (https://commons.wikimedia.org/w/index.php?curid=33820444)

Teamdetourodisha–Own work, CC BY-SA 4.0, (https://commons.wikimedia.org/w/index.php?curid=76547551)

Ilya Mauter–Own work, CC BY 3.0, (https://commons.wikimedia.org/w/index.php?curid=4128442)

Ilya Mauter–Own work, CC BY 3.0, (https://commons.wikimedia.org/w/index.php?curid=4128442)

Walters Art Museum: Home page Info about artwork, Public Domain, https://commons.wikimedia.org/w/index.php?curid=18804797)

Dalbera from Paris, France–Peinture murale avec Shiva (Haveli Kedia, Fatehpur), CC BY 2.0, (https://commons.wikimedia.org/w/index.php?curid=24665005)

Nasir Kachroo/NurPhoto via Getty Images, (https://www.gettyimages.in/detail/news-photo/image-of-lord-shiva-is-seen-on-the-t-shirt-of-a-devotee-news-photo/1158190460)

Acknowledgements

I would like to thank Ananth Padmanabhan for coming up with the idea of the book and for the wonderful title. Even though the book is mine in every sense of the word, it is Ananth who I would like to give the entire credit to—for it is after the seed of this idea was planted by him that I took on this project and nurtured it into a book.

I would also like to thank my two fabulous collaborators, the immensely prolific Johan Mattelaer from the tiny town of Kortrijk, and the elegant Philip Van Kerrebroeck who hails from Antwerp. Both Johan and Philip are experts on the phallus and have written extensively on the same. After many meetings across Ghent, Bruges, Antwerp and Brussels, we came up with the concept behind the book.

However for me, as a writer, the journey was not only both visual and pleasurable, but a deeply spiritual one, too. For me, the phallus belonged to the Indian primordial god, Shiva; and so, while Johan and Philip brought in the magic, fertility, potency and the representation of the phallic culture from Occidental, Oriental and Indigenous societies, I concentrated on the metanarrative of the phallus and the interrogation of the phallus through the lens of the 'lingam'. Seeing the wide scope of the book, I then invited Sudhir Kakar to join us, who in turn, pointed me in the direction of scholar Amrita Narayanan. It was important for me to have within the narrative the psychological imprint of the phallus, and Amrita readily agreed to be a part of this book.

I would also like to thank my publisher, Udayan Mitra, who stood like a rock and was always graciously present. Udayan brought in the delightful editor Bushra Ahmed, who with her very sensitive, intelligent and reflexive editing has very ably edited the book, adding greatly to the robust health of the book.

To my friend, the very creative Gopika Chofla, who laid the very backbone to the design with her design template—I am indebted. Bonita Shimray, who then took the design to another level and gave the book its magnificent design.

Sanjeev Kumar for the endless hours he spent perfecting the design of the book, and finally Jaseya Fazili, who gave the book the necessary outreach.

To my dear friends, Guy and Nathalie Trouveroy in Brussels who connected me to the Belgian Ambassador in India and to Francois Delhaye in helping me showcase my book in the lovely residence of the Belgian Embassy in New Delhi.

I would like to acknowledge the crucial assistance of Dilpreet Bhullar with my writing and Rashmi Kapoor for accessing images. Saurabh Rai and Ravindra Rawat for the many onerous jobs of printouts, photocopies etc. they helped me with.

In the end, my husband Mukul Joshi and my daughter Mandakini Devi for being my emotional pillars of strength, and my father, Jagdish Chandra Pande, who led me to Bhakti Marg.

About the authors

Dr Alka Pande

Dr Alka Pande is a well-known writer, art historian and art curator. Her major fields of interest are gender identity and sexuality, and traditional arts. She has been the recipient of many awards and honors; she was awarded the Knight of the Order of Arts and Letters by the French government in 2006, and the Australian-India Council Special Award for her contribution to Indian art in 2009, to name a few. She has authored many books, such as *Body Sutra*, *Panchtattvas: The Road Ahead*, *Divine Gesture: The Magnificence of Mewar Spirituality*, *Mukhwas: Indian Food through the Ages*, *Shringara: The Many faces of Indian Beauty*, *Leela: An Erotic Play of Verse and Art*, and *The New Age Kama Sutra for Women*, among many others. Currently Dr. Pande is a consultant art advisor and curator of the Visual Arts Gallery at the India Habitat Centre in New Delhi (India).

Philip E.V. Van Kerrebroeck

Philip E.V. Van Kerrebroeck was born in Louvain (B) and followed Greco-Latin Secondary school. He obtained a medical degree from the University of Louvain, and trained in general surgery and urology in Belgium, The Netherlands and the USA. He received a master's degree in medical sciences from the University of Antwerp (B), and a PhD in medicine from the Radboud University of Nijmegen (Nl). Since November 1998, he has been professor of urology at the University of Maastricht (Nl) and received the Emeritus status on 31 October 2020. He is a member of twenty-five scientific societies, and has authored over three hundred and sixty peer-reviewed articles, book chapters and books, mainly in the field of urology, but also dealing with anthropologic topics.

Johan Mattelaer

Johan Mattelaer worked as a urologist in the Department of Urology at AZ Groeninge till 2003. He is an expert on the history of medicine, urology and sexology. He has written and edited many books, such as *The Phallus in Art and Culture*, *From Ornamentation to Mutilation: Genital Decorations and Cultural Operations in the Male*, *Forbidden Fruit: Sex, Erotics and Art*, and *Sexological and Other Less Logical Stories*, to name a few.

Amrita Narayanan

Amrita Narayanan Psy.D. is a clinical psychologist and psychoanalyst in private practice. Amrita read history and French at Middlebury College, Vermont, as an undergraduate, and earned her doctorate in clinical psychology in 2007, from the Stanford University Psy.D. consortium, California. Following this, she trained as a psychoanalyst via the Indian Psychoanalytical Society. Amrita's writing has appeared in academic journals such as *Psychodynamic Practice* and *Psychoanalytic Review*; newspapers such as The *Hindu* and The *Indian Express*; and popular press periodicals such as *Outlook*, *Open Magazine*, and *India Today*. Her most recent work is as editor of *The Parrots of Desire: 3000 years of Erotica in India* (Aleph Book Company, 2018) a collection of poems, short prose and fiction in translation from Indian languages, linked by an introductory essay on the central themes in Indian erotic literature.

First published in India by HarperCollins *Publishers* 2021
HarperCollins Publishers India, Cyber City, Building 10-A, Gurugram, Haryana-122002, India
www.harpercollins.co.in

This edition published in India by HarperCollins *Publishers* 2026

2 4 6 8 10 9 7 5 3 1

P-ISBN: 978-93-6989-120-7
E-ISBN: 978-93-5357-701-8

Designed by HarperCollins *Publishers* India
Printed and bound at Nutech Print Services Pvt. Ltd.

*

HarperCollins Publishers, Macken House, 39/40 Mayor Street Upper, Dublin 1, D01 C9W8, Ireland